Counterfeits At Your Door

JAMES BJORNSTAD

GL
Regal
Books

A Division of G/L Publications
Glendale, California, U.S.A.

Other good Regal reading

So, What's the Difference? by Fritz Ridenour
Will the "Saints" Go Marching In? by Floyd McElveen
Issues and Answers by Gary Maeder with Don Williams

The foreign language publishing of all Regal books is under the direction of *Gospel Literature International* (GLINT) a missionary assistance organization founded in 1961 by Dr. Henrietta C. Mears. Each year *Gospel Literature International* provides financial and technical help for the adaptation, translation and publishing of books and Bible study materials in more than 85 languages for millions of people worldwide.

For more information you are invited to write *Gospel Literature International*, Glendale, California 91204.

Published by Regal Books Division, G/L Publications
Glendale, California 91209
Printed in U.S.A.

Library of Congress Catalog Card No. 78-72864
ISBN 0-8307-0610-0

The publishers do not necessarily endorse the entire contents of all publications referred to in this book.

CONTENTS

A teaching manual and discussion guide for use with this book are available from your church supplier.

99767

Dedicated to my Mother and Father,
who taught me at an early age
what the truth is and
how to discern truth from error.

INTRODUCTION

Many religions, some of them quite new, hand us answers to be accepted in faith. Invariably though, when we try to "spend" these answers in the marketplace of real life we find that we have a counterfeit. In America today there are more than 2,000 religious movements and practices for people to participate in, such as yoga or meditation.

With all of this divergent religious activity commanding attention, seeking converts and claiming to be the truth, it is easy to see how even the Christian, let alone the non-Christian, could become confused. How, in a world of religious diversity and confusion, can we keep from being deceived and accepting the counterfeits? Is it really important that we detect these religious counterfeits?

Consider the customer who goes to his bank with his deposit, only to learn from the teller that one of the bills he has is a counterfeit. He is both shocked and embarrassed to learn that he has received and accepted a counterfeit bill. The bank will confiscate the bill and forward it to the United States Treasury Department, and the customer loses that amount of money.

The person involved in a counterfeit Christian religious movement is in somewhat the same position as the customer. He doesn't like to hear the word "counterfeit." He is no less shocked and embarrassed to learn he has accepted a false religion, one he has been worshiping in and living by, believing it was genuine. The thought of its being false never entered his mind. He is so sure it is the real thing, anyone would have a difficult time trying to tell him, let alone demonstrate to him, that his religious beliefs and experiences are false.

The religious counterfeit must be unmasked. The person must be told because the ultimate penalty for possessing false religious beliefs is infinitely greater than the penalty for possessing counterfeit money. It is eternal separation from God in a place of torment.

When he confiscates counterfeit money, the bank teller feels the effects of detecting the counterfeit and informing the customer. He realizes that, although he can detect counterfeit bills, uninformed people do actually believe in and accept the counterfeit as real. He also has reinforced within him his great responsibility in detecting the counterfeit. For if he fails to do so and accepts the bill as genuine, the bank suffers the loss.

The Christian is in somewhat the same position as the teller. If he has not already identified them, he must become aware of the religious counterfeits in the world today. There is "another Jesus . . . a different spirit" and "a different gospel" (2 Cor. 11:4), and these are accepted and believed to be genuine by those who are uninstructed and spiritually blind. The Christian must realize his role and responsibility in detecting the counterfeit. In doing this, he will first of all keep himself from being deceived and "led astray from the simplicity and purity of devotion to Christ" (2 Cor. 11:3). He can also help the unwary person who possesses counterfeit religious beliefs to discard the counterfeit and false for the genuine and true, thus keeping that person from walking blindly down the steps leading away from God.

Counterfeits are part of our world today, and the acceptance of these, whether money or religious beliefs, results in loss for someone. Therefore, it is important that we detect the counterfeits. To do this we need to know something of the nature of counterfeiting.

How Counterfeiters Work

No one counterfeiting hundred-dollar bills would use 6x3-foot sheets of coarse sandpaper for paper, hot pink ink, or put a picture of Mickey Mouse on the front and Disneyland on the back—at least, not if he wanted to fool people and have his counterfeits accepted as genuine hundred-dollar bills. The counterfeiter takes great pains to mimic every detail in copying. Should any imperfection appear to be noticeable, he will even resort to dipping the bills in coffee and coffee grounds, rubbing them in dirt or mutilating the bills—doing everything possible to reduce the chances of detection and increase the chances of acceptance.

The counterfeiter, of course, knows the bills are fakes. Unfortunately, the people who receive them accept them as real and unsuspectingly pass them to others.

In the religious world Satan is the master counterfeiter. He too knows his products are fakes, and those who receive his counterfeit religious beliefs and experiences accept them as genuine, as from God Himself. They, unaware of the counterfeit, pass it on to others in their proselyting (converting others).

In 2 Corinthians 11 the apostle Paul expresses this problem in declaring that Satan "disguises himself as an angel of light" (v. 14), and those who accept his counterfeits become "false apostles, deceitful workers, disguising themselves as apostles of Christ" (v. 13).

In these same verses the apostle Paul also describes the deadly parallel between pseudo-Christianity (false) and true Christianity, in which he likens the former to a carefully designed copy of the latter.

Pseudo Christian religious movements claim to be genuine—true Christianity. They use Christian terms (such as God, Jesus, saved, etc.), which could easily be construed as being Christian, when actually they mean something different by these words. They also use verses from the Bible to support their beliefs, making them sound very biblical, when in reality the passages have been taken out of context or reinterpreted in light of pseudo Christian beliefs. All of this produces the appearance of being Christian, thus decreasing the chances of their being detected.

Since counterfeits are designed to be deceptive replicas of the genuine, and people do unsuspectingly accept counterfeits in place of the real thing, we not only need to be aware of the counterfeits' existence but we also need to be able to detect them and separate them from the genuine.

Detecting the Counterfeit

The goal of all counterfeiting is to produce the "perfect counterfeit." Of course, such a goal involves a contradiction of terms and categories. If it is perfect, it is genuine and not counterfeit; if it is counterfeit, it is neither perfect nor genuine. All counterfeits are, in some way, different from the genuine and therefore detectable. In order to detect the counterfeit, we need training.

Bank tellers receive about two weeks of training in which they are taught, among other subjects, to detect counterfeit bills. For some, this training is given at a special tellers' school while for others it is part of their on-the-job training with an experienced teller. In either case, the teller handles bills constantly to develop the feel of the genuine. *Knowing the genuine is the most important factor in detecting the counterfeit.*

After a while a few counterfeits, some obvious and one or two not so obvious, are slipped into a stack of bills. At first, the trainee detects only the obvious. Gradually, through continual handling of bills, the teller develops a feel and ability to detect counterfeits.

The primary method in detecting counterfeit bills is tactile—the "feel" quality, which experienced tellers rely on. There are also secondary methods that rely on the visual to detect the counterfeit. This involves noting the quality of the paper, the color of the ink, the quality of the engraving and the composite. For example, in checking the quality of the paper, if a teller receives one of the bills that has been dipped in coffee and coffee grounds or rubbed in dirt, he uses an eraser and rubs on the white area of the bill to see if the paper has red and blue fibers. If it doesn't, it's a counterfeit. In addition to these, tellers are told to check certain important hallmarks which could mark a bill "suspect," such as serial numbers and the different seals.

The goal of religious counterfeits is deception, presenting a likeness to the original while at the same time maintaining differences. Thus they appear to be "Christian" to the unsuspecting and uninformed. In Matthew 24 Jesus declares that "false Christs and false prophets will arise" in the days prior to His return, and that their purpose will be to present a counterfeit version of Him "so as to mislead, if possible, even the elect" (v. 24). So important is this point of deception that Jesus repeats it as a warning three times (vv. 5,11 and 24) in connection with the religious counterfeits that will appear.

As deceptive as they may be, religious counterfeits can be detected. The apostle John warns us "do not believe every spirit, but test the spirits to see whether they are from God" (1 John 4:1). *The crucial test in detecting religious*

10

counterfeits is the person and work of Jesus Christ, a test which John applies in verses 2 and 3 to detect the counterfeits of his day:[1] "By this you know the Spirit of God: every spirit that confesses that Jesus Christ has come in the flesh is from God; and every spirit that does not confess Jesus is not from God" (1 John 4:2,3).

Why are the doctrines of Jesus Christ the crucial test in the detection of religious counterfeits? The apostle John provides the answer. "He who has the Son has the life; he who does not have the Son of God does not have the life" (1 John 5:12).

If the doctrines of Jesus Christ (i.e., His person and work) are perverted, the identity of the Life-Giver is altered. If the identity of the Life-Giver is altered, then the life which He came to give is correspondingly misrepresented.

Furthermore, the apostle John states, "Whoever denies the Son does not have the Father; the one who confesses the Son has the Father also" (1 John 2:23). From this we learn that a person's understanding of Jesus Christ affects his understanding of God, and his relationship to God depends on his relationship to Jesus Christ. The eternal destiny of his soul depends upon his understanding and acceptance of the true Jesus Christ as Lord and Saviour.

It is imperative, therefore, to detect the distortions and perversions in the doctrines of Jesus Christ presented by the religious counterfeits today. Christians need training in this, and that is the purpose of this book.

A Quick Overview

We first must become familiar with the genuine. The first section presents the genuine, the biblical understanding of the person and work of Jesus Christ. The four areas we will focus on are His deity, His humanity, His death and saving sacrifice, and His resurrection. These are the areas to keep in mind in evaluating all religious movements, as they will

11

be the areas in which the counterfeit can be detected.

After focusing on the genuine, we will "slip in some counterfeits," so to speak. The remaining sections will focus on the doctrines of Jesus Christ as presented by two religious counterfeits—the Jehovah's Witnesses and the Church of Jesus Christ of Latter-day Saints (Mormons). These will be tested by the doctrines we studied in the first section to reveal the differences and detect the counterfeits.

It is our prayer that through the study of this material, the reader will become more familiar with the biblical doctrines of Jesus Christ, develop an ability to detect distortions of these doctrines, be able to respond to these distortions with the true teaching from the Bible and be challenged both to live and witness more effectively for the Saviour. Then in that day when we stand before Him we will hear the Master say, "Well done, good and faithful slave ... enter into the joy of your master" (Matt. 25:21, 23).

Reflection

1. Do you really care that people you know and come in contact with are without Jesus Christ and headed for the lake of fire? (See Rev. 21:8.)
2. Why is it important for you to detect religious counterfeits?
3. Are you prepared to detect religious counterfeits? Honestly now, how well do you know the doctrines regarding the person and work of Jesus Christ?
   □ Very well.
   □ I think I could hold my own in a discussion.
   □ It would help me to know a little more.
   □ I really need further study of this.

Thinking Ahead

Suppose you were backed up against the wall and told to

12

prove the deity of Jesus Christ? Could you do it? What passages would you use?

Note

1. In John's day, for example, *Docetism* maintained that Christ only seemed to have a human body and to suffer and die on the cross; and *Gnosticism* preached that matter is evil and freedom from that evil comes only through knowledge of spiritual truth.

WHAT THINK YE OF CHRIST?

What think ye of Christ? is the test
To try both your state and your scheme;
You cannot be right in the rest
Unless you think rightly of Him.
As Jesus appears to your view,
And He is beloved or not,
So God is disposed to you—
And mercy or wrath is your lot.

Some take Him a creature to be—
A man, or an angel at most,
But they have not feelings like me,
Nor know themselves wretched and lost;
So guilty, so helpless am I,
I durst not confide in His blood,
Nor on His protection rely—
Unless I were sure He is God.

John Newton

SECTION I

BEFORE YOU OPEN THE DOOR

Meet the biblical Jesus

1. Jesus' Deity
2. Jesus' Humanity
3. Jesus' Death and Saving Sacrifice
4. Jesus' Resurrection

1

JESUS' DEITY

Two thousand years ago the greatest person who ever lived was born in a stable in the small and obscure village of Bethlehem in Palestine. His name was Jesus Christ.

His birth was no ordinary event. Despite the fact that He was not born into a famous or wealthy family, news of His birth was heralded far and wide. Nearby shepherds were told by the angel, "Today in the city of David there has been born for you a Savior, who is Christ the Lord" (Luke 2:11). In a distant land wise men learned of His birth from a star and traveled a great distance to worship the child who had been born (see Matt. 2:1-11). When news of Jesus' birth reached Herod, the reigning monarch, he attempted to destroy Him by killing all the infants "from two years old and under, according to the time which he had ascertained from the magi" (Matt. 2:16). Even Herod realized that Jesus was no ordinary child.

His birth was no ordinary birth. Two parents are needed

for conception to produce a child, but this was not the case in Jesus' birth. He was conceived by the power of the Holy Spirit in the womb of His virgin mother, Mary, without male participation (see Matt. 1:18-25; Luke 1:26-38).

His birth produced no ordinary human being. Prior to coming to earth, Jesus was with God and He was God (see John 1:1). Notice that John 1:1 says that there is more than one person in the Godhead (i.e., the Being we call "the one true God") and that Jesus is one of these. In time and space He "became flesh, and dwelt among us" (John 1:14). The phrase, "became flesh" or "came in the flesh," implies Jesus' preexistence as God, which verse 1 declares. While He was here on earth Jesus was given the name *Immanuel*, because He is "God with us" (Isa. 7:14; Matt. 1:23). Jesus Christ, who had His existence eternally within the unity of the Godhead, became man without giving up His oneness with God. He truly was God in human flesh.

Different from All Others

From the very beginning of His ministry, Jesus Christ was different from all His contemporaries. There was something extraordinary about Him.

The people noted the difference. In a synagogue in Capernaum Jesus casts out a demon from a man and all who are present are amazed. "What is this?" they ask. "A new teaching with authority! He commands even the unclean spirits, and they obey Him" (Mark 1:27). Later in Capernaum He tells a paralytic, "My son, your sins are forgiven" (Mark 2:5). The scribes ponder, "Why does this man speak that way? He is blaspheming; who can forgive sins but God alone?" (Mark 2:7). Jesus heals the paralytic and all the people remark, "We have never seen anything like this" (Mark 2:12). On still another occasion, when Jesus turns back the storm and calms the sea, the multitude ask one another, "Who then is this, that even the wind and the sea obey Him?" (Mark 4:41).

The disciples noted the difference. Jesus' use of "I say to you" was in marked contrast to the familiar "Thus saith the Lord" which permeated the messages of the Old Testament prophets. (See the Sermon on the Mount where this contrast is stated nine times in the early part: Matt. 5:18,20,22,26,28,32, 34,39 and 44.) In stating this Jesus put Himself in the place of God; His disciples could not miss the meaning of this. Later, when Jesus asked His disciples, "But who do you say that I am?" they knew who He was. Simon Peter answered, "Thou art the Christ, the Son of the living God" (Matt. 16:15,16).

The Jews noted the difference. They soon recognized that He was affirming His equality with God. Once on a Sabbath, Jesus healed a man. When challenged about His working on the Sabbath, Jesus said that His Father was also working (see John 5:17). This so riled the Jews that they "were seeking all the more to kill Him, because He . . . was calling God His own Father, making Himself equal with God" (John 5:18). On another occasion Jesus said, "I and the Father are one" (John 10:30). When the Jews took up stones to stone Him, He asked them for which good work they were going to stone Him. They said, "For a good work we do not stone You, but for blasphemy; and because You, being a man, make Yourself out to be God" (John 10:33).

There can be no doubt that the people in Jesus' day knew He was different from all others. They knew He did things and made claims no mere human being could. Even His enemies realized this. They resorted to all kinds of explanations, calling Him demonic (see John 8:48) or accusing Him of blasphemy (see Mark 14:64) rather than accepting the obvious conclusion that He was God in human flesh.

Divine Claims

From the very beginning of His ministry Jesus Christ claimed equality with God in very clear and unmistakable statements.

He equated a person's attitude to Himself with the person's attitude to God. He told people that—

• in seeing Him, they were seeing God (see John 14:9);
• in knowing Him, they were knowing God (see John 8:19);
• in believing in Him, they were believing in God (see John 12:44);
• in receiving Him, they were receiving God (see Mark 9:37);
• in honoring Him, they were honoring God (see John 5:23);
• in hating Him, they were hating God (see John 15:23).

He equated Himself with Jehovah by using the Old Testament title, "I Am"[1] (see Exod. 3:13,14; Deut. 32:39; Isa. 43:10). The Jews were quite familiar with "I Am." When Jesus claimed this for Himself, they knew what He meant and they reacted strongly, even seeking, on occasion, to kill Him for this. Consider the following:

• After telling the Jews He was from above, Jesus continued to say, "Unless you believe that I Am, you shall die in your sins" (John 8:24).
• Speaking of His forthcoming crucifixion, Jesus said, "When you lift up the Son of Man, then you will know that I Am" (John 8:28).
• When the Jews scorned the thought that Abraham had seen Jesus, Jesus said, "Truly, truly, I say to you, before Abraham was born, I AM" (John 8:58).
• In declaring His omniscience (His having complete knowledge) to His disciples, Jesus said, "From now on I am telling you before it comes to pass, so that when it does occur, you may believe that I Am" (John 13:19).
• Jesus' claim to be "I Am" caused the mob to draw back and fall to the ground (see John 18:6).
• In response to the high priest's question, "Are You the Christ, the Son of the Blessed One?" Jesus said, "I Am; and you shall see the Son of Man sitting at the right hand of

19

Power, and coming with the clouds of heaven" (Mark 14: 61,62). The high priest's response indicates that he understood Jesus' use of "I Am" as a claim to His deity.

Jesus equated Himself with Jehovah by identifying Himself as the Jehovah of the Old Testament. On one occasion Jesus was doing many miracles but the people were not believing in Him. Jesus made reference to Isaiah 6, where Isaiah entered the presence of Jehovah seated on His throne. Jesus applied this passage to Himself. "These things Isaiah said, because he saw His [Jesus] glory, and he spoke of Him [Jesus]" (see John 12:41). Jesus was saying that Isaiah saw Him on the throne. He was Jehovah.

On another occasion Jesus said, "Your father Abraham rejoiced to see My day; and he saw it, and was glad" (John 8:56). When did Abraham see Jesus? Could this be a reference to Jehovah's appearing to Abraham on the plains of Mamre (see Gen. 18), in which case Jesus was saying that He was Jehovah?

There are many other single references in which Jesus sets Himself forth as deity. When they are combined there can do no doubt of Jesus' claim to equality with God.

Divine Attributes

From the very beginning of His ministry Christ demonstrated His claim to deity by doing what God can do.

• Jesus demonstrated His deity in knowing the thoughts and intents of men (see Matt. 9:4; 12:25; Luke 6:8; 9:47).

• Jesus demonstrated His deity in forgiving sins, which only God can do (see Mark 2:5,7; Luke 7:48,49).

• Jesus demonstrated His deity in seeing events occur while being far removed (see John 1:48-50).

• Jesus demonstrated His deity in healing people (see Matt. 8:2-4,5-13,14-17; 9:20-22; 12:9-13; Mark 2:3-12; 7:32-37; Luke 17:11-19; 22:47-51; John 5:1-9; 9:11).

• Jesus demonstrated His deity in raising the dead, (see Matt. 9:18-26; Luke 7:11-15; John 11:1-44).

• Jesus demonstrated His deity in controlling nature and its elements (see Matt. 14:22-33; Mark 4:35-41; John 2:1-11; 6:1-14).

At every step in His life we are confronted with demonstrations of His deity which verify His claim to be God in human flesh.

Jesus Is Worshiped

The divine claims of Jesus Christ and His demonstrations of divine attributes lead us to worship Him as deity. If He is who He claims to be, and He demonstrated this through His abilities, then He is to be worshiped. That is exactly what we find in the Bible.

From the very beginning of His ministry Jesus Christ allows Himself to be worshiped. This is clear and unmistakable evidence of His claim to be God, for we are all commanded to worship only God (see Deut. 6:13; Matt. 4:10).

To worship any other as God, whether angel, man or man-made image is idolatry. In Colossians 2 we are warned, "Let no one keep defrauding you of your prize by delighting in . . . the worship of the angels" (Col. 2:18). We are not to worship angels and this is consistently demonstrated throughout the Bible. In Revelation 19:10 an angel (see 18:1) refuses worship from John. In Revelation 22:8,9, an angel refuses John's worship a second time, saying, "Do not do that . . . worship God."

Furthermore, Romans 1 explains that fools "exchanged the glory of the incorruptible God for an image in the form of corruptible man" (Rom. 1:23). Obviously, we are not to worship man either. This, too, is consistently demonstrated throughout the Bible. In Acts 10:25,26, Peter refuses worship from Cornelius. In Acts 14:11-15, Paul and Barnabas refuse worship at Lystra.

From this evidence we can conclude that neither angels nor men are to be worshiped. Yet Jesus is worshiped, as we shall see, because He is God. He is not an angel or mere

21

man. He is God, and God alone is to be worshiped.

In Matthew, where Jesus Himself refuses to worship Satan, stating, "You shall worship the Lord your God, and serve Him only" (Matt. 4:10), the worship set forth throughout that book is specifically to Jesus Christ.

- The wise men worship Him (see Matt. 2:2,11).
- A leper worships Him (see Matt. 8:2).
- A synagogue official worships Him (see Matt. 9:18).
- The people in the boat worship Him (see Matt. 14:33).
- The Canaanite woman worships Him (see Matt. 15:25).
- The mother of the sons of Zebedee worships Him (see Matt. 20:20).
- His disciples, after His resurrection, worship Him (see Matt. 28:9,17).

There are many other passages which we could focus on, all stating that Jesus is worshiped or that He is to be worshiped. Some of these are the following:

- Men worship Him (see John 9:38).
- The disciples worship Him (see Matt. 28:9,17).
- The saints in glory worship Him (see Rev. 5:1-14; 7:9-17).
- The angels worship Him (see Heb. 1:6).
- One day everyone will bow before Him (see Phil. 2:10, 11).

There is no doubt in the Bible that Jesus is worshiped. Because of this, the only possible conclusion we can come to is that Jesus not only claims to be, but actually is God in human flesh.

Jesus Is Jehovah

Further support for Jesus Christ's divine claims and attributes is presented throughout the Bible. Whatever is said of Jehovah is said of Jesus. Whatever is claimed for Jehovah is claimed for Jesus. Consider a few of these:

- Both Jesus and Jehovah are the "Mighty God" (cf. Isa. 10:21; Isa. 9:6).

- Both Jesus and Jehovah are the "I Am" (see Exod. 3:14; cf. John 8:58).
- Both Jesus and Jehovah are the "First and Last" (see Isa. 41:4; 44:6; cf. Rev. 1:17; 2:8).
- Both Jesus and Jehovah are the Creator (see Gen. 1:1; Isa. 40:28; cf. John 1:3; Col. 1:16; Heb. 1:8-12).
- Both Jesus and Jehovah are the Saviour (see Isa. 43:3,11; 45:21,22; cf. John 4:42; Acts 4:12).
- Both Jesus and Jehovah are confessed as Lord (see Isa. 45:24; Joel 2:32; cf. Rom. 10:9-13; Phil. 2:10,11).
- Both Jesus and Jehovah are worshiped (see Gen. 24:26, 52; Ps. 2:11; cf. Matt. 2:2,11; John 9:38).
- Both Jesus and Jehovah are prayed to (see Num. 11:2; 1 Sam. 1:10,12,26,27; cf. Acts 7:59).
- Both Jesus and Jehovah are the Shepherd (see Pss. 23; 100; Isa. 40:11; cf. John 10:11; Heb. 13:20; 1 Pet. 5:4).
- Both Jesus and Jehovah are King (see Jer. 10:10; Isa. 44:6; Ps. 47:2,6,7; cf. Matt. 2:2; Luke 23:3).

A study of these can only lead us to the same conclusion repeated throughout this chapter: The Bible fully supports the fact that Jesus is Jehovah as He claimed. He is God in human flesh.

Second Person of the Trinity

From the very beginning of His ministry, Jesus Christ continually spoke of the Father, a separate Being, who obviously is God. He tells us the Father was the one who sent Him and whose will He came to do (see John 5:30; 6:38,39,40). He even prayed to the Father (see John 17:1, 24,25). But Jesus also spoke of the Holy Spirit, interrelating this personal Being with Himself and the Father (see John 14; 16; 17). How, then, do we understand the relationship of Jesus Christ, whom we have already seen is God and is to be worshiped, with the Father who also is God and is to be worshiped? How does the Holy Spirit fit into this relationship? This brings us to the doctrine of the Trinity.

The word Trinity does not occur in the Bible. It was developed in the early church to express the doctrine of God presented in the Bible. The word trinity is a shortened form of tri-unity, indicating three-in-oneness. There is no finer descriptive term of the one God revealed in the Scripture as Father, Son and Holy Spirit.

The Bible teaches there is but one God (see Deut. 6:4; 1 Cor. 8:4). God Himself states, "Is there any God besides Me . . . ? I know of none" (Isa. 44:8). The apostle Paul tells us that though there are many things which are called gods (see 1 Cor. 8:5; Gal. 4:8), there is by nature only one true God (see Deut. 6:4; 1 Cor. 8:4,5; Gal. 4:8).

In the Bible the Father is presented as that one true God (see Gal. 1:1). As we have seen, Jesus Christ is also presented as that one true God (see John 1:1; 5:18; 10:30). The Holy Spirit is presented as that one true God (see Acts 5:3,4). Here we have three distinct persons, each presented as being the one true God of the Bible.

Therefore, God is one God and three persons are that one true God. There is both unity and plurality in the Godhead, which can be expressed as three-in-one or tri-unity—Trinity.

The Old Testament contains evidence for the plural nature of the Godhead and, therefore, for the Trinity. The following pairs of verses show a pattern of using the plural and the singular in referring to God:

"Let us make man in our image, according to our likeness" (Gen. 1:26). "And God created man in His own image" (Gen. 1:27). The "us" and "our" in verse 26 can only be the one God of verse 27.

"Come, let Us go down and there confuse their language" (Gen. 11:7). "So the Lord scattered them abroad" (Gen. 11:8).

The three-in-oneness which is God, Jesus, and the Holy Spirit in one Godhead, is the reason for the changing plural and singular of these verses.

We also find evidence for the Trinity in the New Testament. The resurrection of Jesus Christ from the dead is a good example of this. In 2 Corinthians 4:14; God "raised the Lord Jesus." In Galatians 1:1, "God the Father ... raised Him from the dead." In John 2:19, speaking of His body, Jesus said, "In three days I will raise it up." In John 10:17, Jesus explained, "I lay down My life that I may take it again." In Romans 8:11, the Holy Spirit "raised Christ Jesus from the dead." Who raised Jesus from the dead? The only sensible answer is God the Father, Son and Holy Spirit.

Prayer is another example. Contrary to some teaching, which declares that we are to pray only to God the Father, the New Testament mentions prayer to all three persons of the Trinity. In Luke 6:12 prayer is offered to God. In Matthew 6:9 prayer is offered to the Father. In Acts 7:59, prayer is offered to Jesus. In Acts 13:2 prayer is evidently offered to the Holy Spirit since He speaks to the church leaders. Who is prayer to be offered to? Again, the only sensible answer is God the Father, Son and Holy Spirit.

Further evidence of the three persons of the Godhead can be seen in the New Testament. At Jesus' baptism, all three persons were present (see Matt. 3:16,17). Jesus tells the disciples to baptize in the name (singular of the Father, Son and Holy Spirit (see Matt. 28:19). Paul's blessing includes the "grace of the Lord Jesus Christ, and the love of God, and the fellowship of the Holy Spirit" (2 Cor. 13:14).

From our study we can now conclude that Jesus Christ is the second Person of the Triune (three-in-one) God, equal in dignity, majesty, glóry and power with the Father and the Holy Spirit. He is deity and as such deserves our worship and allegiance.

Reflection
1. What does the fact that Jesus is God mean to you?
2. Suppose you were one of the disciples actually with

Jesus throughout His ministry. Make a list of things you heard and saw that proved to you that Jesus Christ is God.

Projects and Proofs

1. Develop a presentation on the deity of Jesus Christ. Be sure to include passages that clearly state His deity, ones you can explain in some detail. Focus on the real issues of who Jesus is and what that should mean to the individual you are presenting this to. Practice this entire presentation with someone, perhaps a friend or family member.

2. Do the same for the doctrine of the Trinity.

Thinking Ahead

Suppose you were in the middle of an argument among your friends. Some are saying that Jesus is God and others claim that He was only a man. You realize that Jesus is God and that He came to earth and lived a human life 2,000 years ago. How would you explain this?

_____

Note

1. The *New American Standard Bible* includes the word "He" although it is not in the original text. The Jews and the disciples understood it in the absolute sense of "I Am," referring to Jesus' claim to be God.

2

JESUS' HUMANITY

Have you ever wondered why the humanity of Jesus Christ is so important to the Christian faith? Why does it matter that Jesus really was a human being, not just seeming to be human, appearing and disappearing as a ghost? Part of the answer lies in the fact that God doesn't deal in counterfeits. It took a real human person to do what Jesus did for us, not just an apparition or a symbol, and God loved us so much that He sent His only Son as that person, not just another messenger (see John 3:16).

Jesus Christ, before coming to planet earth, was the eternal Word of God, the second Person of the Triune God, co-equal, co-existent, and co-eternal with the Father and the Holy Spirit. The apostle John tells us that this one who "was" from all eternity, (see John 1:1), "became flesh, and dwelt among us" (John 1:14).

The apostle Paul expresses in great detail what actually happened. Jesus Christ, who "existed in the form of God, did not regard equality with God a thing to be grasped, but emptied Himself, taking the form of a bond-servant, and being made in the likeness of men. And being found in appearance as a man, He humbled Himself by becoming obedient to the point of death, even death on a cross" (Phil. 2:6-8).

Note carefully that Jesus Christ possessed all the essential attributes of deity from eternity. Equality with God was not something He had to grasp or hold on to; it was His because of His deity. However, He willingly added to Himself the essential attributes of man, including a human body. Furthermore, He left His heavenly setting for the setting and circumstances of mankind.

In His coming to earth Jesus Christ retained His essential attributes of deity. (In the last chapter we noted some of the demonstrations of these attributes.) But in His "taking the form of a bond-servant, and being made in the likeness of men," He added this human nature to His divine nature, blending them into one personality. In doing this He limited Himself, choosing not to exercise all of His divine attributes in His humanity. But He never ceased to be God while adding to Himself a genuine human nature and living a genuine life here on earth.

A Real Man

None of His contemporaries doubted or denied that Jesus Christ was a real man. Though His conception was supernatural, His nine-month existence in His mother's womb and His birth prove that His humanity was genuine (see Luke 2:6,7).

Eight days after His birth He was circumcised just as any other Jewish male baby would be (see Luke 2:21). Mary also went to the Temple to have the purification ceremony, which was required after childbirth, performed for her (see Luke 2:22-24). It was here that Simeon, who had been told by God that he would not die until "he had seen the Lord's Christ" (Luke 2:26), took Jesus in his arms and blessed

28

God, saying, "Now Lord, Thou dost let Thy bond-servant depart in peace, according to Thy word; for mine eyes have seen Thy salvation" (Luke 2:29,30). The prophetess Anna also recognized Jesus' special mission of redemption (see Luke 2:36-38).

Not much is known of the next 11 years of Jesus' life. We can infer that it was during this time He learned His father's trade of carpentry. Apart from this and other inferences, all we have in the Bible is a summary of His growth and development given by the physician Luke: "And the Child continued to grow and become strong, increasing in wisdom; and the grace of God was upon Him" (Luke 2:40).

At age 12 Jesus traveled to Jerusalem to attend the Passover with His mother and father. This was probably in preparation for His bar mitzvah the following year (age 13), when He would be permitted to join the religious community as a responsible member. After the seven-day festival, Mary and Joseph returned. However, unknown to them, Jesus remained in Jerusalem. When they went back to find Him, He was "in the temple, sitting in the midst of the teachers, both listening to them, and asking them questions" (Luke 2:46).

Notice here that at this age Jesus already knew who He was and why He had come into the world. He said to Mary and Joseph, "Why is it that you were looking for Me? Did you not know that I had to be in My Father's house?" (Luke 2:49). This was not something He learned from Mary and Joseph, because "they did not understand the statement which He had made to them" (Luke 2:50). So it did not come from them.

Luke summarizes the next 18 years or so of Jesus' life, up to the beginning of His public ministry, by writing, "Jesus kept increasing in wisdom and stature, and in favor with God and men" (Luke 2:52).

The public ministry of Jesus lasted only a few years and yet, even during this time, we can see various physical and emotional experiences that point to His humanity. There are many examples of these in the Gospels:

- Jesus returned weakened and hungry from His temptation in the wilderness (see Matt. 4:2,11).
- He was tired from traveling (see John 4:6).
- He needed sleep (see Matt. 8:24).
- On more than one occasion He was angry with those who defiled His Father's house (see John 2:14-17; Matt. 21:12,13).
- He was aggravated with those who refused the truth of God (see Mark 3:5).
- He was "deeply moved" (see John 11:33) to the point of tears (see John 11:35) at the tomb of His dear friend Lazarus.
- He wept for the city of Jerusalem (see Luke 19:41).
- He was deeply troubled as He anticipated His death on the cross (see John 12:27).
- His earthly life, like all other human lives, was terminated by death (see John 19:33,34).

Perhaps a note on the death of Jesus Christ is in order here. When Jesus died, He died as a man. As it is with all human beings, the body died. The soul and spirit continued to exist. In Jesus' case His body died, but His divine nature continued to exist. His physical resurrection is proof that He continues to exist now.

There can be no doubt that Jesus Christ was a genuine human being. His development from infancy to adulthood followed the normal course of maturity in every respect. Not only were His physical growth and strength pictured as normal, but so were His intellectual and emotional development. Therefore, He was not only God while He was here, He was true man as well.

Change in Setting

The relationship between God the Father and the second Person of the triune God changed when the second Person added to Himself the nature of man and became man. While God the Father and God the Holy Spirit still operated from heaven, the Word was no longer in heaven; He was here in the person of the Lord Jesus Christ.

This is why John's Gospel begins with the fact of the Word's eternal existence, being with God and being God (see John 1:1). When the Word "became flesh" (John 1:14), it meant His relationship with the Father and the Holy Spirit would now be from earth. The remainder of the Gospel takes place in this framework: Jesus here on earth relating to the Father in heaven, and vice versa.

We would misunderstand the life and statements of Jesus Christ if we failed to comprehend this new setting for the interrelationships of the Persons of the Trinity. Failure to comprehend this framework has led to some of the greatest challenges to the truth of the deity of Jesus Christ.

A Father-Son Relationship

In this new setting we see a beautiful father-son relationship. Something of the oneness of and intimacy between the persons of the Godhead is expressed in Jesus Christ being called the "beloved Son" of God. Of all mankind He was the most precious in the Father's sight. He was so special that at the beginning of His ministry, when He was baptized, God Himself intervened from heaven, calling attention to the fact that Jesus was His "beloved Son" (Luke 3:22). Later in Jesus' ministry, God spoke again, this time at the transfiguration of Jesus. He declared, "This is My beloved Son, with whom I am well pleased" (Matt. 17:5).

Furthermore, Jesus referred to Himself as "the Son" (see Matt. 11:27) and to God as "the Father" (see John 5:19) or "My Father" (see Matt. 7:21). In Jewish thought, "son of" implies equality and identical nature. Thus, when Jesus said He was the "Son of God," He identified Himself as God and equal with the Father in an unqualified sense. The Jews understood this and accused Him of blasphemy (see

31

John 19:7). Similarly, when Jesus implied His sonship, and thereby His deity, by calling God His "Father," the Jews promptly accused Him of "making Himself equal with God" (John 5:18).

Jesus Christ is also called the "only begotten Son." In Jewish thought "only begotten" denotes "uniqueness" or "one-of-a-kind-ness." Jesus was God's only Son, loved by the Father above everyone and everything.

Jesus Christ is also called the "first-born" (see Col. 1:15). In Jewish thought this means "first right," referring to position and rank. It includes having the preeminence and becoming the rightful heir by declaration of the person's father rather than because of order of birth. Jesus is given this position and rank by the Father. He is the preeminent One. His primacy and supremacy are clear in His relationship to the created universe (see Col. 1:15); to the resurrection of the dead (see Col. 1:18; Rev. 1:5); and to His people who, through Him, become part of God's family (see Rom. 8:29). He is also the rightful "heir of all things" (Heb. 1:2).

Seeing this new framework, then, we see Jesus as the only Son, the second Person of the Godhead, here on earth as the unique and preeminent one, precious and loved in the Father's sight.

A God-to-God Relationship

In this new setting Jesus Christ calls His Father "God" and "My God." We can see this in His high-priestly prayer, when He prays "that they may know Thee the only true God" (John 17:3); in His cry on the cross, "My God, My God, why hast Thou forsaken Me?" (Matt. 27:46); and in His words to Mary following His resurrection, "I ascend to My Father and your Father, and My God and your God" (John 20:17).

Here we have one person of the Godhead talking to another person of the Godhead, or God talking to God. Such communication between the persons of the Godhead is recorded on other occasions in the Bible. For example, "The LORD says to my Lord: Sit at My right hand, until I make Thine enemies a footstool for Thy feet" (Ps. 110:1). Jesus, in commenting on this passage, asked the questions, "How does David in the Spirit call Him 'Lord,'" and, "If David then calls Him 'Lord,' how is He his son?" (Matt. 22:43,45). The conclusion Jesus is driving home to the Pharisees is that the Messiah is deity. The rest of Psalm 110 demands the same conclusion. Psalm 110:1 is presenting communication between two persons of the Godhead.

Logically it should pose no problem that Jesus, one person of the Godhead, called the Father, another person of the Godhead, "God." They are both God. Furthermore, in identifying Himself with man and speaking from the position of His humanity, even though He was deity, it was appropriate for Jesus in this new setting to call the Father in heaven "My God."

A Subordinate Relationship

In His humanity, Jesus is subject to the Father. Jesus Himself, speaking to the disciples, says that "the Father is greater than I" (John 14:28; cf. 10:29). This relationship demonstrates that He is willing to do the Father's will, even though He has authority and powers.

We see here something of the working order within the Trinity in which God the Father has a different function or role from God the Son. Since these functions or roles are within the Godhead, it cannot mean Jesus is any less deity.

Consider the president of the United States. Within the populace of this country he is greater than we are by virtue of his position, authority and recognition. But since it is a function and role within the realm of human beings, it surely does not mean that he is more than human or that we are less than human.

Another passage indicating the same relationship is 1 Corinthians 11:3, where Paul says, "But I want you to understand that Christ is the head of every man, and the man is the head of a woman, and God is the head of Christ." In this passage, man is referred to as "the head of woman" in illustration of Christ's headship in relation to us and God's headship in relation to Christ. In the man/woman relationship, neither is more important, but they are subject to one another in love (see Eph. 5:21). This same equality but loving submission is expressed in the father-son relationship of God and Christ: Christ willingly does the Father's will. In so doing, He expresses His humanity in terms we can understand, the terms of a loving family relationship. As man and woman are both human, the wife chooses to submit to her husband out of love, (see Eph. 5:22,23), so God and Christ are both deity, and Christ chooses to submit to God's will during His life on earth. Paul uses a family relationship, then, to explain the relationship between God and Christ.

We see the same subordination in 1 Corinthians 15:23-28, where Paul states that there is a day coming when Jesus will purposely and knowingly shift the focus of attention from Himself as Saviour, Intercessor and Lord to full focus on the Father. At that time, says Paul, "the Son Himself also will be subjected to the one who subjected all things to Him, that God [i.e., the triune God] may be all in all." Since both the Father and the Son are God, this passage predicts another shift in the working order in the Godhead.

We can conclude, then, that with Jesus here on earth the Father has a different function from that of Jesus, and Jesus willingly subordinates Himself to the will of the Father, without in any sense violating His own true deity or humanity.

Self-Limitation
In becoming man and partaking of human conditions, Jesus Christ limited His exercising some of His divine attributes. For example, in taking to Himself a human body

He limited His omnipresence (ability to be present in all places).

Jesus also limited Himself in the manifestation of His "glory." He prayed, "And now, glorify Thou Me together with Thyself, Father, with the glory which I ever had with Thee before the world was" (John 17:5). Note the statement by Jesus "which I ever had *with* Thee." There can be no doubt that Jesus is referring to His deity and His divinely inherent glory, for Jehovah's glory will not be given to any person other than Jehovah (see Isa. 42:8; 48:11). But this prayer also states that Jesus was not continually manifesting His inherent glory of God because of His humanity. However, He did manifest it on certain occasions, such as on the Mount of Transfiguration (see Matt. 17:2) and it was clearly seen and understood by His disciples. The apostle John, who had been an eyewitness of this, states: "We beheld His glory, glory as of the only begotten from the Father" (John 1:14).

Furthermore, He limited Himself in His omniscience. In speaking to His disciples about the time of His return, He said, "of that day or hour no one knows, not even . . . the Son, but the Father alone" (Mark 13:32). It is important that after His resurrection, when asked about "restoring the kingdom to Israel," He did not say, "I do not know." He said, "It is not for you to know times or epochs which the Father has fixed by His own authority" (Acts 1:7).

Jesus demonstrated His omniscience during His ministry, as we noted in the last chapter; however, apparently He chose not to exercise it on this one occasion. The fulfillment of these things was a matter that lay within the Father's sole authority, was not the concern of the disciples, and was not for Jesus to reveal.

We can conclude from this that Jesus Christ deliberately limited Himself as a man in order to be truly human. These self-imposed limitations should not be interpreted as weaknesses or imperfections, but should be recognized as the

35

logical outgrowth of the incarnation, His becoming flesh.

The God-Man

As we have seen, Jesus Christ is both God and man, and we must see both of our Lord's natures in their proper relationship with each other. To say He is only God is to say He is not human and thus He cannot sympathize with our weaknesses (see Heb. 4:15). To say He is only man is to say He is not God and thus God was not "with us" (see Matt. 1:23).

Jesus Christ is neither all God nor all man. His divine attributes were interwoven with His human nature. Without question He was a genuine human being but He was also much more than a mere man. He was genuine deity, too. He was the God-Man, second Person of the triune God in human flesh.

We should also keep in mind that being God is not the same as being a perfect man. Even if a man could be perfect as Jesus was (which man cannot do because of sin—see Rom. 3:23), he would still be only a perfect man and not God. Jesus Christ was true man, but He was more; He was also true God and that is something we can never be.

Reflection

1. Had you ever considered before what actually happened when Jesus left heaven for earth? Is it important? Why?
2. Write a newspaper headline and a feature article on Jesus coming from heaven to earth. Write out what happened when Jesus added to Himself a human existence.

Projects and Proofs

Make a list of passages that, because of Jesus' humanity, appear to contradict His deity. Write a response for each of these. Be sure to include material from this chapter as well as from other sources.

Thinking Ahead

A friend makes it quite clear that she believes Jesus died, but that His death was nothing more than any other human death. Do you agree with her? If not, how is the death of Jesus Christ greater than anyone else's death?

3

JESUS' DEATH AND SAVING SACRIFICE

Imagine the impact on the disciples if, at the end of His work on earth, Jesus Christ simply disappeared, avoiding the most feared event of human existence—death. Many of His claims would suddenly have seemed just words, and the magnificent meaning of His sacrificial death would have been lost. Anything less than His sacrificial death would have made His claims a counterfeit, and God does not hand us counterfeits.

Jesus Christ, the second Person of the triune God, willingly left His heavenly setting, added to Himself a human nature and entered the setting of earth. It was not by chance that He came. He had a specific purpose for coming which He revealed on several occasions. To some of His disciples He said He "did not come to be served, but to serve, and to give His life a ransom for many" (Mark 10: 45). He told Zaccheus that the purpose of His coming was "to seek and to save that which was lost" (Luke 19:10). To the Pharisees He spoke of Himself as the good shepherd who "lays down His life for the sheep" (John 10:11,14,18).

The main purpose of His coming was clearly redemptive in nature. He entered a world where the relationship between God and His people was broken by sin so that He could forgive and restore each one of us to the loving relationship God first intended. According to Romans 3:23, "All have sinned and fall short of the glory of God." Moreover, Romans 6:23 explains that "the wages of sin is death." However the second Person of the Godhead, Jesus, became a man so He could lay down His life on Calvary's cross in our place—to pay for our sin. His death made it possible for those who trust in Him as Lord and Saviour to be reconciled to God and forgiven of sins.

His redemptive work, which saved us from the eternal penalty for sin and reunited us with God, cannot be understood apart from His being both God and man. Only God can forgive sins. Therefore, if Jesus was not truly God, He could not be our Saviour and could not forgive our sins. If He did not truly become a man, He could not die for our sins. Being God qualified Him to be our Saviour, but His atoning (substitutionary) death for us in His humanity actually made Him our Saviour.

A proper understanding of the person of Jesus Christ is essential to a proper understanding of the nature of His redemptive work. The fact that Jesus is God means that His redemptive work is exclusively God's accomplishment and provision. "God was in Christ reconciling the world to Himself" (2 Cor. 5:19). Because it is God's doing, it cannot be man's doing. It is not God's redemptive work *plus* something, but His redemptive work *alone*.

A proper understanding of the person of Jesus Christ— His nature and attributes—is essential to understanding the effectiveness of His redemptive work. The fact that Jesus is God means that His redemptive work is not for one time, place, or situation. It has infinite and eternal value. It is available to all people of all times in history. To have an atonement of such infinite worth requires an infinite sacrifice, a sacrifice of a magnitude that only the God-Man could provide. No mere man could provide this.

A proper understanding of the person of Jesus Christ is also essential to our receiving and experiencing His redemptive work. The fact that Jesus is God means that one cannot have the benefits of the redemptive work of Jesus and at the same time reject Jesus' deity. Jesus explained this in very blunt fashion to the Jews: "You shall die in your sins; for unless you believe that I am [i.e., deity], you shall die in your sins" (John 8:24)

From this we see that the redemptive work of Jesus Christ cannot be fully understood apart from His nature as God and man.

Jesus, Our Sacrifice for Sin

To understand the significance of Jesus' death and what it accomplished, we need to look at the Old Testament sacrificial system. In Old Testament times, an animal was slaughtered and its blood placed on the altar. This was God's appointed way for man, separated from God by sin, to receive forgiveness for sins and be reconciled to God. And yet the *blood* of animals was not able in itself to cleanse from sin, as the author of Hebrews states, "It is impossible for the blood of bulls and goats to take away sins" (Heb. 10:4). Neither was the *act* of sacrificing these animals to God able to cleanse man of sin: "And every priest stands daily ministering and offering time after time the same sacrifices, which can never take away sins" (Heb. 10:11).

What, then, did the sacrificial system provide? It provided a temporary forgiveness for sin which people accepted by faith, and made it possible for them to be accepted by God. But more than this, the shedding of blood and the provision of a life offered in the sinner's place,

40

emphasized the need for a substitutionary sacrifice.

Jesus Christ made the final infinite blood sacrifice on the cross, for all sin, offering Himself in our place as the substitutionary sacrifice. The author of Hebrews says His coming was "to put away sin by the sacrifice of Himself" (Heb. 9:26). "He, having offered one sacrifice for sins for all time, sat down at the right hand of God . . . there is no longer any offering for sin" (Heb. 10:12,18).

Because of Jesus' sacrifice, the sin that separates us from God is forgiven if we believe in Jesus, and we can be reconciled to God—that is, we can have fellowship with Him again.

Thus, those who by faith offered sacrifices in the Old Testament looked *forward* to the cross and believed that one would come to provide the ultimate atonement. We by faith look *back* to the cross and to the One who died there in our place as our sacrifice for sin.

Jesus, Our Passover Lamb

To understand the significance of Jesus' death and what it accomplished, we need to look at the Passover, which was first celebrated at the time of the Exodus. The Israelites were in Egypt for 400 years, part of that time as slaves to the Egyptians. God, in the process of forcing Pharaoh to let the people leave Egypt to go to their own land, sent nine plagues, showing His power to Pharaoh. The last plague was the death of all the first-born in the land of Egypt. In order to be spared, the Israelites had to sacrifice a lamb without blemish (see Exod. 12:5), kill it (see Exod. 12:6) and put its blood around the wood supports of their door (see Exod. 12:7). The blood was a sign. And when the Lord saw it on the doorposts He passed over that household and did not take the life of their first born (see Exod. 12:13).

In the Passover we can again see the substitutionary sacrifice and appropriation of its benefits by faith (see Heb. 11:28). The New Testament teaches that Jesus fulfilled all that the Passover Lamb represented. The apostle Paul says He is our Passover (see 1 Cor. 5:7). Peter declares Him to be the "lamb unblemished and spotless" (1 Pet. 1:19) and John the Baptist, upon seeing Jesus, identifies Him in this fashion: "Behold, the Lamb of God who takes away the sin of the world!" (John 1:29). Because we are, by faith in Jesus, covered by His blood, the angel of eternal death will pass over us (see John 11:26).

Jesus, Our Suffering Messiah

To understand the significance of Jesus' death and what it accomplished, we also need to look at the suffering Messiah presented in Isaiah 53. Here we see that the Messiah "would render Himself as a guilt offering" (Isa. 53:10).[1] He would provide Himself as the sacrifice. He would be the sin-bearer. We can also see that His death would be a substitutionary death, one "in place of" others. He would not die for His own sins but for the sins of others. Isaiah says, "Surely *our* griefs He Himself bore, and *our* sorrows He carried . . . He was pierced through for *our* transgressions, He was crushed for *our* iniquities . . . the Lord has caused the iniquity of *us* all to fall on Him . . . He will bear *their* iniquities" (Isa. 53:4,5,6,11, italics added by author).

From this we can conclude that the Old Testament clearly points to the need for an ultimate sacrifice for sin, since the Old Testament sacrifices were never able to redeem us in themselves. It also tells of the One who would provide that ultimate sacrifice and atonement once and for all time by His substitutionary death: Jesus Christ, who "gave Himself up for us, an offering and a sacrifice to God" (Eph. 5:2). It was He who "bore our sins in His body on the cross" (1 Pet. 2:24), reconciling us to God "through the blood of His cross" (Col. 1:20).

Jesus, the Ultimate Atonement

Though we cannot understand completely the redemptive work provided by Jesus Christ, the New Testament does present various ideas to explain and illustrate the meaning and significance of His death on Calvary's cross.

We can see the element of substitution in His redemptive work. Because of sin, we all deserve death (see Rom. 3:23; 6:23). But Jesus died in our place. "For Christ also died for sins once for all, the just for the unjust, in order that He might bring us to God" (1 Pet. 3:18).

We can see the element of reconciliation in His redemptive work. Because of sin, we have been separated from God who is holy and righteous. But Jesus died to remove the root cause of this alienation—sin—thus bringing together the two parties and reconciling us to God. For "while we were enemies, we were reconciled to God through the death of His Son" (Rom. 5:10).

We can see the element of ransom in His redemptive work. We have been captured by sin and held in its power. But Jesus died to provide a ransom, meeting all of the holy requirements of God's law and its curse, and redeeming us from the power of sin (see 1 Tim. 2:6).

Because of sin we have offended God and raised His anger. But in His redemptive work Jesus died to turn away the wrath of God from us by the offering of Himself. Jesus is "the propitiation for our sins" (see 1 John 4:10).

We can see the element of completion in His redemptive work. On the cross Jesus cried, "It is finished!" (John 19:30). Jesus has already done everything necessary for our salvation. He has lived the life we could never live and His death paid the price for all our sin. As John states, "The blood of Jesus His Son cleanses us from all sin" (1 John 1:7). It is true that we still need daily cleansing and forgiveness of sin (see 1 John 1:9) as we go through life, but we receive forgiveness on the basis of what has already been accomplished by Jesus Christ. His death once and for all time paid the price for all sin—past, present and future.

In the New Testament we see God's love demonstrated

for us in the person of Jesus Christ. "We know love by this, that He laid down His life for us" (1 John 3:16).

Obtaining the Benefits

As we have seen, through the death of His Son on Calvary's cross, God provided redemption for our sins. He has accomplished it all. The question before us now is how we can appropriate His redemptive work and experience its benefits.

The Bible makes it clear that redemption is not appropriated by everyone. Jesus Himself said, "Not every one who says to Me, 'Lord, Lord,' will enter the kingdom of heaven" (Matt. 7:21). Some will hear from Jesus, "Depart from Me, accursed ones, into the eternal fire which has been prepared for the devil and his angels" (Matt. 25:41). Not everyone will be saved.

The Bible makes it clear that we do not appropriate redemption by our efforts and abilities. Paul says it is "not of yourselves . . . not as a result of works, that no one should boast" (Eph. 2:8,9).

The Bible also makes it clear that we do not appropriate redemption by keeping the Law—the Ten Commandments. Paul says, "A man is not justified by the works of the Law . . . since by the works of the Law shall no flesh be justified" (Gal. 2:16).

If our efforts, abilities and achievements do not make it easier or possible for us to benefit from Jesus' redemptive work, what does? The Bible makes it clear that we appropriate it only "through faith in Christ Jesus" (Gal. 2:16). We are justified on the basis of what Jesus has accomplished and His authority to forgive and to declare right before God those who have faith in Him (see Gal. 2:16; Eph. 2:8,9).

Note the repeated emphasis on faith in Christ. Jesus Christ's nature and attributes cannot be fully understood apart from His redemptive work. It is faith in Christ our

Redeemer—the One who has accomplished redemption—
that saves.

In summary, salvation is a free gift, which can be appropriated by everyone who by faith accepts Jesus Christ as
Lord and Saviour (see Acts 16:31; Rom. 6:23). This involves not just acknowledging the redemption, but putting
one's life in His hands. Jesus said, "He who believes in the
Son has eternal life; but he who does not obey the Son shall
not see life, but the wrath of God abides on Him" (John
3:36).

Determining One's Eternal Destiny

Whether or not one has appropriated the redemptive
work of Jesus by faith in Him as Lord and Saviour determines one's eternal destiny. Those who accept Him are
assured of an eternal relationship with Him. Those who
reject Him are eternally separated from Him and will be
cast into the lake of fire, a place of torment (see Matt.
8:11,12; 13:40-42,49,50; 2 Pet. 2:17; Jude 13; Rev. 20:13,
14).

In Luke 16:19-31 Jesus clearly reveals the difference in
existence after death between those who by faith accepted
Him and those who rejected Him. Eternal salvation for the
believer is contrasted with eternal damnation of the un-
believer (see Matt. 25:46), and existence in one state or the
other is based solely on acceptance or rejection of the person and work of Jesus Christ.

In conclusion, Jesus Christ is the second Person of the
triune God, the One who loved us so much that He left
heaven, adding to Himself a human nature in order to lay
down His life for our sins so that we, through faith in Him,
might live forever with Him in the everlasting fellowship of
the redeemed. "There is salvation in no one else; for there
is no other name under heaven that has been given among
men, by which we must be saved" (Acts 4:12). He is "our
great God and Savior" (Titus 2:13).

Reflection

1. Jesus died. What does His death mean to you? What has it done for you?
2. Have you personally put your trust in Jesus Christ and accepted Him as your Saviour?
3. Is it important to your salvation that Jesus Christ is deity? Why?
4. If you were to stand right now before Jesus Christ and He asked you why He should let you go into His heaven, what reason would you give Him?

Projects and Proofs

Write some poetry or lyrics for a song or even a television commercial expressing all that Jesus has accomplished for you in His death on Calvary's cross.

Thinking Ahead

You happen to stumble upon a program on television in which the participants are discussing the resurrection of Jesus Christ. The prevailing position seems to be against His resurrection. You feel like jumping in to straighten them out. What would you say? What evidence would you give for the resurrection of Jesus Christ?

Note

1. The Jews expected an earthly king, based on this passage. Actually, the prophecy pointed to a heavenly King and Saviour.

4

JESUS' RESURRECTION

Jesus Christ is the second Person of the triune God who added to Himself a human nature and lived here among men as deity incarnate (in human form). On one occasion He chased out of the Temple the money-changers and those who sold animals, charging them with desecrating His Father's house. Of course, to the Jews, claiming God as your Father made you equal with God, and so they challenged Him to "prove it." He responded by declaring His forthcoming resurrection from the dead as His proof (see John 2:14-22).

From Jesus' statement we can see that the validity of the person of Jesus Christ as God depends upon the historical fact of His resurrection from the dead. This is the "primary proof" that He was indeed who He claimed to be—"the Son of God" (see Rom. 1:4). Had He failed to rise from the dead as He said He would, His claim to deity would have been disproved.

Jesus Christ came to die on the cross for our sins—to pay

our penalty for sin (separation from God). However, if He had simply died, then He would have been conquered by the last enemy—death, which is the result of sin (see Rom. 6:23). His redemptive work would remain unfinished. This is why Paul can say, "If Christ has not been raised [bodily], your faith is worthless; you are still in your sins" (1 Cor. 15:17). Thus Jesus' ultimate victory over sin was His triumph over death in His resurrection. This proved Him to be truly God, more powerful than death, and the unique redeemer who is able to give us resurrection life.

From this we can see that the resurrection of Jesus Christ from the dead is an integral part of His person and redemptive work. They cannot be separated. As such it is also an integral part of salvation itself, so much so that God bases eternal salvation on acceptance of this fact. "If you confess with your mouth Jesus as Lord, and believe in your heart that God raised Him from the dead, you shall be saved" (Rom. 10:9).

His Resurrection Foretold

The Old Testament records a number of prophecies concerning Jesus' resurrection from the dead. Not only the Old Testament but Jesus Himself stated that He would rise again.

Psalm 16:8-11 is one example where Jesus' resurrection is foretold. This passage is cited in Acts 2:31. Here Peter, speaking on the day of Pentecost, says the fulfillment of the Old Testament passage could not have been David because "he both died and was buried, and his tomb is with us to this day" (Acts 2:29). If it was not David, then who does it refer to? Obviously, the one who has already risen from the dead—Jesus Christ. Peter says that David, being "a prophet . . . looked ahead and spoke of the resurrection of the Christ" (Acts 2:30,31). Jesus, then, was the fulfillment of this Old Testament prophecy given hundreds of years before His time.

There is further evidence that the Old Testament foretold Jesus' resurrection. Several New Testament writers explained the life, death and resurrection of Christ as fulfillment of Old Testament prophecy. For example, we know on one occasion, Paul reasoned with those in the synagogue "from the Scriptures, explaining and giving evidence that the Christ had to suffer and rise again from the dead" (Acts 17:2,3). ("Scriptures" at that time referred to what is now the Old Testament.) Further Old Testament prophecy of Christ's redemptive suffering is seen in Isaiah 53:1-6.

We can also see Jesus foretelling His own resurrection in the Gospels. Early in His ministry we find Jesus telling the Jews, "Destroy this temple, and in three days I will raise it up" (John 2:19). John gives us the meaning of Jesus' statement: "He was speaking of the temple of His body" (John 2:21). Thus it is a prophecy of His forthcoming resurrection. Later in His ministry—after Peter's great confession—Matthew records that Jesus "began to show His disciples that He must go to Jerusalem, and suffer many things . . . and be killed, and be raised up on the third day" (Matt. 16:21). In fact, Jesus rarely spoke of His coming death without also predicting His resurrection after three days (see Matt. 17:22,23; 20:18,19; 26:31,32).

These prophecies not only state who would be resurrected (Jesus, the Messiah), but also the exact time of His resurrection (the third day after His death), and the mode of resurrection (bodily).

"He Is Risen!"

Jesus' prophetic statements that He would arise from the dead on the third day were so fantastic that His disciples did not believe it—until it actually happened! On the third day, exactly as Jesus said, He rose from the dead. The hard factual evidence of seeing the prophecy fulfilled for themselves made the disciples believe it. John says, "When therefore He was raised from the dead, His disciples

49

remembered that He said this; and they believed the Scripture, and the word which Jesus had spoken" (John 2:22).

There can be no doubt that Jesus died. His crucifixion took place publicly in Jerusalem during the Passover, one of the greatest Jewish religious festivals. His trial, conviction and sentence were conducted under the direction of the Roman governor and his soldiers, working in cooperation with the Jewish authorities. He was pronounced dead by the Roman soldiers (see John 19:31-35), embalmed in about one hundred pounds of bandages and spices (see John 19:39,40), and interred in a guarded tomb (see John 19:41,42; Matt. 27:57-66). On the third day He emerged from the grave victorious over death, leaving His tomb empty for all to see (see Matt. 28:1-6; Mark 16:1-8; Luke 24:1-9; John 20:1-9). He then proceeded to demonstrate the fact of His resurrection to many people:

• First Sunday morning—He appeared to Mary Magdalene (see John 20:11-18); He appeared to the women (see Matt. 28:1-10; Luke 24:1-11); He appeared to Peter (see Luke 24:34; 1 Cor. 15:5);

• Sunday afternoon—He appeared to the two disciples on the Emmaus road (see Luke 24:13-35);

• Sunday evening—He appeared to the disciples, minus Thomas (see John 20:19-25).

• Next Sunday—He appeared to the disciples, including Thomas (see John 20:26-29).

• Next four to five weeks—He appeared to James (see 1 Cor. 15:7); He appeared to the disciples at the Sea of Tiberias or Galilee (see John 21:1-23); He appeared to about 500 brethren at one time (see 1 Cor. 15:6). He appeared to the disciples on a mountain in Galilee (see Matt. 28:16-20); He appeared to the disciples in Jerusalem (see Luke 24:48-53; Acts 1:3-8).

These resurrection appearances of Jesus cannot be explained away. The collective evidence and the diverse nature of His appearances to people place His resurrection beyond illusion, delusion and doubt. Jesus was seen by many people on at least 10 different occasions over a period of 40 days. He was seen in the morning, afternoon and evening. He appeared to Mary when she was alone, to the disciples together in a group and to a crowd of more than 500. With some He walked and talked along the road and accompanied them to their house, (see Luke 24:28-30). On occasion He stayed long enough to teach about the Kingdom (see Acts 1:3).

His appearances were greeted with a variety of responses. His disciples were frightened, thinking they had seen a spirit (see Luke 24:37), while Mary was overwhelmed with emotion (see John 20:11-17). Thomas couldn't buy the story that Jesus had risen from the dead . . . until he saw Him. At that moment when Jesus appeared to him, he worshiped Him (see John 20:28).

The facts of history recorded in the Gospels demand the conclusion that Jesus Christ rose from the dead. There is no other conclusion possible that will fit all of the facts.

Physical Resurrection

There also can be no doubt that Jesus Christ anticipated His resurrection in a physical form. He said, "Destroy *this* temple [His body], and in three days I will raise *it* up" (John 2:19, italics added). This was fulfilled in His bodily resurrection from the grave, in which He triumphed over the destiny of all bodies—the grave—and showed us that Christians shall also receive new heavenly bodies at the resurrection.

He appeared to the witnesses noted previously and presented His body for all to see and examine. To Thomas, who could not understand the resurrection, Jesus offered His hands and His side bearing the wounds of the cross as tangible evidence of His bodily resurrection (see John 20:24-29). On another occasion, He appeared to His disciples, "They were startled and frightened and thought that they

51

were seeing a spirit." Jesus, perceiving their fear, said, "Why are you troubled, and why do doubts arise in your hearts?" And then, to correct their mistaken perception, He said, "See My hands and My feet, that it is I Myself; touch Me and see, for a spirit does not have flesh and bones as you see that I have." To further prove His physical nature, He asked, "Have you anything here to eat?" Luke recorded that "they gave Him a piece of a broiled fish; and He took it and ate it in their sight" (Luke 24:36-43).

This is proof of the physical nature of His resurrection body and also indicates that it was the same body in which He had been crucified. However, in His resurrection appearances we can also see that His resurrected body is different from His previous body in that it was capable of passing through obstructions of matter, such as closed doors (see John 20:19). Although the body of Christ after His resurrection was not subject to the same physical limitations as before, His resurrection body was the same body and was no mere ghost. He was tangible.

There are those who, while accepting the resurrection of Jesus Christ from the dead, deny the fact that He rose bodily from the dead. They point to the fact that neither Mary Magdalene (see John 20:11-18) nor two of the disciples (see Luke 24:13-31) recognized the risen Jesus. From this they deduce that Jesus had no identifiable form and that He must have been a spirit. Well, in Mary's case the mere mention of her name brought her out of her emotional situation. But in the case of the two disciples, Luke tells us the reason they did not recognize Jesus was that "their eyes were prevented from recognizing Him" (Luke 24:16). Jesus prevented them from learning His identity until He had taught them certain things and stimulated their faith. The moment that their "eyes were opened . . . they recognized Him" (Luke 24:31).

These same people also argue that Jesus was raised as a spirit from the dead by referring to Peter's statement of

52

Jesus "having been put to death in the flesh, but made alive in the spirit" (1 Pet. 3:18). However, the latter part of this verse should more accurately be translated "made alive by the spirit." Romans 8:11 is complementary to this passage, telling us that it was by the Holy Spirit that Jesus was raised from the dead.

We can conclude from the evidence, then, that Jesus Christ rose bodily from the dead as He said He would. However, there's more!

He Ascended

Jesus' post-resurrection appearances to His disciples did come to an end. The time came for Jesus to leave His earthly setting for heaven, as He had prophesied He would to His disciples on several occasions (see John 14:3; 16:17). So He met with His disciples on the Mount of Olives and finally physically departed from them. His physical form was lifted up in full view of His disciples and received into a cloud (read Acts 1:1-11). Thus, His earthly ministry was victoriously concluded. However, Jesus sent the Holy Spirit, the third Person of the Trinity to be with His followers always, as He promised (see John 14:16-19; 16:7-18; Matt. 28:18-20; Rom. 8:9-11). Jesus, being God is also with us as He promised.

He Is Coming Again

The very same one who rose bodily from the dead and ascended into heaven is going to return one day. Just as surely as He ascended on high, He will come again, and in the same manner. As the two angels told those who watched Jesus ascend on high, "This Jesus, who has been taken up from you into heaven, will come in just the same way as you have watched Him go into heaven" (Acts 1:11).

Yes, Jesus will return bodily and visibly to this earth. In His bodily resurrection He has accomplished total redemption for man (both spiritual and physical) and His bodily return to earth will bring about this completion in the lives of His children (see Rom. 8:23,24; 1 John 3:2,3). Furthermore, His return will bring about the fulfillment of His plan for the ages, a new heaven and new earth "wherein dwells righteousness."

Conclusion

We have seen that Jesus Christ is deity, the second Person of the triune God. All of the attributes of deity were His. In His incarnation He never ceased to be God while adding to Himself a genuine human existence. However, since His incarnation He has—and will never cease to have—all the essential attributes of humanity. He has identified Himself with humanity forever, and it is with Him that we who love Him and have accepted Him as Lord and Saviour will enjoy eternal blessedness.

We have also seen that the person of Jesus Christ cannot be separated from His redemptive work. But neither can His bodily resurrection be separated from His person and His redemptive work. Salvation is thoroughly intertwined with His deity, His humanity, His death and His bodily resurrection from the dead. To deny any one of these elements affects the whole doctrine of Jesus Christ and correspondingly negates the salvation which He offers.

Reflection

1. If Jesus never rose from the dead, would it make any difference as far as you are concerned? Why?
2. What does His bodily resurrection provide for you?
3. Does it make any difference whether Jesus rose from the dead in physical form or a spirit? Why?

Projects and Proofs

Make a list of evidences you could use to support the biblical claim that Jesus Christ rose in physical form from the dead. Use material from this chapter.

Check List

☐ Is God triune—three Persons in one God?

☐ Is Jesus Christ the second Person of the triune God?

☐ Did Jesus Christ live a genuine human life here on earth?

☐ Is the death of Jesus Christ on the cross sufficient in itself to pay for all sins?

☐ Is salvation by faith in Jesus Christ alone?

☐ Did Jesus Christ arise bodily from the dead?

SECTION II

JEHOVAH'S WITNESSES AT YOUR DOOR

The person and work of Jesus Christ according to the Jehovah's Witnesses

5

MEET THE JEHOVAH'S WITNESSES

Your doorbell rings. You answer it, finding two people supplied with a magazine called *Awake* or *Watchtower* and a prepared speech. They want you to accept their literature. How are you going to respond?

Before you can respond, you need to know something about the religious movements and beliefs these people represent. There is a counterfeit at your door. That means there is an opportunity at your door.

Jehovah's Witnesses claim to be the oldest line of "true" worshipers of God. They trace their lineage directly back to Adam and Eve's second son Abel,[1] who "offered to God a better sacrifice than Cain, through which he obtained the testimony that he was righteous" (Heb. 11:4). This is the earliest reference Jehovah's Witnesses use in what seems to be a desire to trace a history of people who, like Abel, have been "true" witnesses to Jehovah.

According to Jehovah's Witnesses, these "true" witnesses to Jehovah became scattered in time and were without a leader. Drawing on this dispersed group,[2] Charles Taze Russell organized a remnant of "true" worshipers in Pittsburgh, Pennsylvania in 1870.

Russell and his followers claimed that they had the sole true interpretation of the Bible, and considered themselves custodians of the divine plan. They had a special preconceived theology and they studied the Bible from that point of view. In 1876 Russell was elected as the "pastor" of this Bible study, and from that time on he was known to his followers as Pastor Russell. He began to publish a semimonthly magazine in 1879 called *Zion's Watchtower and Herald of Christ's Presence*, of which *The Watchtower* magazine today is a descendant. Incorporating in 1884 in the commonwealth of Pennsylvania, the Millenial Dawn (the original name of Russell's group) became Zion's Watch Tower Tract Society. Two years later Russell began to publish a series of volumes entitled *Studies in the Scriptures*. According to Russell, these books contained the essence of the Bible to such an extent that no one could understand the Bible without them.[3]

Russell was the driving force behind the founding of the movement which is known today as the Jehovah's Witnesses. His organizational abilities and energetic preaching and lecture tours brought many converts into the Zion's Watch Tower Tract Society. When Russell died on October 31, 1916, the administration of the society fell into the hands of the executive committee, which consisted of three members: Vice President Ritchie, Secretary-Treasurer VanAmbaugh and Legal Advisor Rutherford. Prior to becoming legal advisor to the Watch Tower, Rutherford had been a trial lawyer and a special judge in the absence of the regular judge of the Eighth Judicial Circuit Court of Boonville, Missouri (the reason for his being known to all as Judge Rutherford).[4] On January 6, 1917 Joseph Franklin Rutherford was unanimously chosen to succeed Russell as president.

Rutherford brought about many changes. In 1929 he condemned all attempts to find God's will outside of the Bible, and in so doing, he disapproved of several of Russell's teachings—for example Russell's theory about the Great Pyramid. (In *Thy Kingdom Come*, Russell had proposed that certain measurements in the Great Pyramid in Egypt would reveal the whole history of mankind as well as the time of the return of Jesus Christ.) At the international convention at Columbus, Ohio in 1931, Rutherford gave the members of the Watch Tower the name by which they are known today—Jehovah's Witnesses.[5] In 1933 he challenged the Roman Catholic Pope to a debate and later challenged the Federal Council of Churches of Christ in America.[6]

Rutherford's prolific writing (over a hundred books and pamphlets), his vigorous attacks upon the doctrines of "organized" religion, and his dynamic leadership caused the Jehovah's Witnesses to grow both in influence and number.

When Rutherford died on January 8, 1942 only five days passed before Nathan Homer Knorr was unanimously elected to succeed him.[7] Knorr was not as spectacular as his two predecessors. However, his concern for training and education, and his strong emphasis on world mission work and individual evangelism brought the increase the Jehovah's Witnesses have seen.[8] New textbooks and doctrinal books were written and published by the society during this time, along with a translation of the Bible favorable to their preconceived theology—*The New World Translation of the Christian Scriptures.* At the time of his death on June 8, 1977 there were 2,248,390 active Jehovah's Witnesses in the world.

On June 22, 1977 at the joint meeting of the boards of directors, Vice President Frederick W. Franz was unanimously elected to succeed Knorr as fourth president in the history of the Jehovah's Witnesses.

Throughout their history, the Jehovah's Witnesses have

60

stressed certain ideas in the proselyting and training of their members which you should know about when speaking to them.

Reason—The Criterion for Truth

The founder of the movement, Charles Taze Russell, stated that the basis for his theology was "reason ... Then we have endeavored to build upon that foundation the teachings of Scripture."[9]

A brief study of the literature of the Jehovah's Witnesses today, as well as most discussions with them, will reveal that reason is still the foundation of their theology and the one criterion by which any Bible doctrine is measured. For example, Jehovah's Witnesses reject the doctrine of the Trinity in the beginning of their booklet, *"The Word" Who Is He? According to John*, because they themselves admit they "cannot scientifically calculate" the Trinity. Furthermore, they claim that "any trying to reason out the Trinity teaching leads to confusion of mind."[10] Thus they reject the Trinity because they claim it is not "reasonable." (Perhaps rather than trying to reason God out they should note His words in Isaiah 55:8,9.)

For the Jehovah's Witnesses, human (and fallible) reason builds the basis for theology and the Bible is made to fit it. Then, all doctrine is tested by reason, and accepted or rejected accordingly.

Furthermore, Jehovah's Witnesses are taught to use reason to attack the beliefs of others in conversation.[11] For example, if you mention that Jesus Christ was deity incarnate they will reason with you that if Jesus was both God and man, such a mixture of two natures would only corrupt both, producing a demigod. "It's the same as mixing red paint with green paint and getting brown paint," said one Jehovah's Witness.

It is important for you as a biblical Christian to keep in mind that you are facing a theology that claims to use reason as its foundation and test for all truth. Therefore you must be able to demonstrate from Scripture itself what the Bible claims to be and teaches, for it alone is the basis and test for all truth.

A Preconceived Theology

Using reason as the basis, Jehovah's Witnesses have developed a preconceived theology into which the Bible must fit—that is, they have first decided what is "logical" to believe and then twisted or changed Scripture so it supports those beliefs. For this reason the founder of the movement, Charles Taze Russell, also taught his followers that "people cannot see the divine plan in studying the Bible by itself."[12] He claimed that his *Studies in the Scriptures* were indispensable to true Bible study and that without his preconceived theology one could not understand the Bible.

Though Jehovah's Witnesses do not make such a bold statement in public today, there has been virtually no change in this attitude since Russell's day. Their literature does set forth a preconceived theology from which they study the Bible, and reason is still the foundation.[13] They still believe that no matter how sincere or diligent you are in your study of the Bible, you walk in darkness apart from the Watchtower Society.[14]

The Watchtower Society claims to be God's channel of communication today,[15] and that communication, when put into written form, produces literature which is free from doctrinal error. Jehovah's Witnesses must accept without question the interpretation of Scripture presented in the literature. (Disfellowshiping or excommunication would be the penalty for any disagreement.) Therefore, they rely exclusively on the Watchtower Society for all doctrinal interpretations; that alone is what they accept as truth. And so the Bible is studied in this "light."

Jehovah's Witnesses will claim that the Bible is the infallible inspired Word of God and the only source and authority for truth. But they do not actually rely on the Bible itself for the truth. Whatever you mention will be filtered through their preconceived theology based on Watchtower literature, and what does not agree with it will be rejected. For example, if you mention the deity of Jesus Christ, that idea will be rejected because their theology contains the belief that Jesus is the first and greatest created being, but not Jehovah God. *They may reinterpret the words you use* and tell you, "We're not denying Jesus is divine. He is powerful and God-like. He is a god." But you will never hear that He is equal to Jehovah God.

Because of their preconceived theology, *they will also interpret differently the Bible passages that you use*—in fact they will reinterpret or change them. If you mention John 10:30 ("I and the Father are one") as proof of Jesus' deity, they will tell you that Jesus is referring to His "oneness in purpose" with the Father, and not to His "oneness in essence," or His deity.

It is important for you to keep in mind that you are facing a narrow preconceived theology which is based on human reason and which uses and misuses biblical passages for support. Therefore you must be able to demonstrate from the Scripture itself what the Bible teaches.

Reflection
1. In considering the preconceived theology of the Jehovah's Witnesses and their stress on reason as the test for truth, what kind of response can you expect when you share your faith with Jehovah's Witnesses?
2. How can you prepare to present God's Word to Jehovah's Witnesses?

Thinking Ahead
Suppose a former classmate (a very good friend of yours) arrives back in town. He calls you to see if he can come over and share his new faith. On the telephone he keeps talking

63

about serving Jehovah, and mentions that Jesus is a created being. Your friend is coming over shortly. How are you going to share your faith with him? How will you show him that Jesus really is God? What Scripture will you use?

Notes

1. *New Heavens and a New Earth* (1953), p. 91.
2. For a fuller biography of Charles Taze Russell, see *Qualified to be Ministers* (1955), pp. 297-312 and *Jehovah's Witnesses in the Divine Purpose* (1959), pp. 14-63.
3. *The Watchtower* (September 15, 1910), p. 298.
4. For a fuller biography of Joseph Franklin Rutherford, see *Qualified to be Ministers*, pp. 312-332 and *Jehovah's Witnesses in the Divine Purpose*, pp. 64-195.
5. *Jehovah's Witnesses in the Divine Purpose*, pp. 125,126.
6. J.F. Rutherford, lectures entitled "Religious Intolerance Why?" published in his book *Intolerance* (1933) and "Jehovah's Witnesses: Why Persecuted?" published in his book *The Crisis* (1933).
7. For a fuller biography of Nathan Homer Knorr, see *Qualified to be Ministers*, pp. 332-345 and *Jehovah's Witnesses in the Divine Purpose*, pp. 196-295.
8. The results of his vigorous evangelistic campaigns can be found by comparing the succeeding editions of the *Yearbook of Jehovah's Witnesses* during his tenure in office.
9. Charles Taze Russell, *Studies in the Scriptures*, ser. 1 (1907), pp. 10,11.
10. *"The Word" Who Is He? According to John* (1962), p. 7.
11. See *Theocratic Aid to Kingdom Publishers* (1945), pp. 212-215.
12. *The Watchtower* (September 15, 1910), p. 298.
13. *E.g.,* "Our obligation is to back up what is said herein by quotations from the Bible for proof of truthfulness and reliability." *Let God Be True* (1952 Revised Edition), p. 9.
14. In a court trial in Scotland in 1954, leaders of the Jehovah's Witness including the president and vice-president admitted under oath that Jehovah directly guides them in interpreting the Bible (see pp. 22-24) and that any person who has only the Bible and not their material is not able to interpret the Bible truly (pp. 133, 499). *Douglas Walsh* v. *Right Honourable James Latham Clyde M.P., P.C. as representing Minister of Labour and National Services*, Court of Sessions, Edinburgh, Scotland, November 23, 1954.
15. See Charles Taze Russell, *op. cit.*, 7th ser. (1917), p. 144 and *The Watchtower* (July 15, 1960), p. 439.

ramp# 6

WHAT DO
THEY SAY
ABOUT
JESUS?

Is the Watchtower Society a counterfeit? Jesus' own question to the Pharisees is an excellent measure: "What do you think about the Christ?" (Matt. 22:42). Jehovah's Witnesses, realizing that this is a crucial question, do not merely dismiss it. They respond with the seemingly thorough but disjointed doctrine of the person of Jesus Christ contained in their literature.

The first president of the Watchtower, Charles Taze Russell, summarizes the person of Jesus Christ in this manner: "When Jesus was in the flesh he was a perfect human being; previous to that time he was a perfect spiritual being; and since his resurrection he is a perfect spiritual being of the highest or divine order."[1]

The literature of the Jehovah's Witnesses today sets forth the same doctrine of the person of Jesus. It claims Jesus Christ has existed in three different, separate states. He was the archangel Michael in heaven before he appeared on earth;[2] he was a man and nothing more than a man while he was here on earth;[3] he is the archangel Michael now in heaven.[4] Let's look at these three stages in some detail.

Jesus, Originally Michael?

Jehovah's Witnesses believe that there was a time when Jesus did not exist. He was the first creation of Jehovah and the only being created directly by him.[5] Jehovah's Witnesses say this is why Jesus is called "the only begotten Son of God."[6] They teach that being the "beginning of the creation of God" means that Jesus was the first of many spirit-sons. Thus he was the brother of Lucifer, another spirit being, who became Satan after his fall. Jehovah's Witnesses claim Jesus was the chief agency through which Jehovah brought all other things into existence. In heaven he was known not as Jesus Christ but as Michael—chief of the angels or the archangel.[7] He was also known as the Word or Logos, which means "one who speaks for Jehovah." As the chief executive officer of Jehovah he could be called a god, a mighty one[8]—but not God!

According to the Jehovah's Witnesses, although Jesus is superior to all other creatures, he is neither eternal nor equal with the Father. They emphatically deny his full deity. He is the Father's first creation and nothing more— Michael the archangel.

Jesus, a Perfect Man

Jehovah's Witnesses believe that Michael the archangel gave up his God-like characteristics in heaven. All that was left was his "life force." Jehovah then took this "life force" of Michael ("personality" or "life pattern" as some call it), and transferred it from heaven to the womb of the virgin Mary.[9] Jesus was miraculously conceived. He was born as a perfect human being,[10] and thus the perfect second Adam.

Since the Jehovah's Witnesses do not believe that Jesus

is God, they do not believe his birth is the incarnation or enfleshment of God. The second president of the Watchtower, Joseph Franklin Rutherford, writes: "Some insist that Jesus while on earth was both God and man in completeness. This theory is wrong, however."[11] Although they do believe that before he came to earth Jesus was a created angel, they deny that Jesus was the incarnation of an angel. In Jehovah's Witness theology there is no incarnation whatsoever.[12] Nothing became flesh. The birth of Jesus meant that he ceased existing as an angel "He laid aside completely his spirit existence."[13] (According to Jehovah's Witnesses there is no continuity between Michael and Jesus despite the fact that Michael's life force was used in the conception of Jesus.) Jesus then began to exist as a man and he was nothing more than a man.

Jehovah's Witnesses claim that Jesus Christ lived a perfect life here on earth and proved himself sinless. He was adopted by Jehovah as a son at his baptism. Once he passed the test of devotion to Jehovah in the temptations with Satan, he began his ministry to proclaim the good news that the kingdom of God was at hand. By his deeds and his faithfulness, he proved himself to be Jehovah's chief witness. When Jesus died, he was annihilated. As a human being he was simply blotted out of existence. He just ceased to exist.

In summary, according to the Jehovah's Witnesses, there was no incarnation involved in Jesus' birth. Though born of the virgin Mary, he was nothing more than a perfect human being when here on earth. His human life was ended by death.

Jesus, Michael Again?

Jehovah's Witnesses believe that after the death of Jesus, nothing existed for three days, then Jehovah raised Jesus from the dead as an immortal spirit.[14] Note carefully that there is no continuity between the human Jesus and the resurrected spirit. Charles Taze Russell, the first president of the Jehovah's Witnesses, once stated that "the man Jesus is dead, forever dead."[15] Therefore, His "resurrection" is actually a "recreation" of his former invisible state as an angel.[16] He became Michael the archangel again, only this time as a divine immortal spirit.[17]

As an angel he (Jesus/Michael) materialized a body resembling the one in which he died so that he could show himself alive to his disciples and prove that he had been resurrected. For 40 days following his recreation he materialized bodies as angels before him had done (for example, see Gen. 19:1-25).[18] In this angelic state he ascended into heaven,[19] where he waited about 1900 years until the end of the "times of the Gentiles."[20] Since Jesus/Michael is a spirit being, his "return" was invisible and took place in 1914. (He did not actually return to this earth, but merely began ruling his kingdom from heaven.)

According to the Jehovah's Witnesses, then, there is nothing human in Jesus' existence after his death. Though he materialized human bodies as proof of his resurrection, he is nothing more than an angel now immortal. He has continued to be and will forever be an angel.

A Disjointed View of Christ

This doctrine reveals a disjointed view of Christ, even though Jehovah's Witnesses seem to portray continuity between the various states of existence. According to the Jehovah's Witnesses, the one who laid down his life at Calvary for our sins was not the one who existed in heaven and had been the Father's agent in creation. Furthermore, he was not the one who was raised from the dead and who now rules in heaven over his kingdom.[21]

What a marked contrast to the words of Jesus Christ Himself. "*I* am the first and the last, and the living One; and *I* was dead, and behold, *I* am alive forevermore" (Rev. 1:17,18, italics added). Furthermore, the author of Hebrews states that "Jesus Christ is the same yesterday and today, yes and forever" (Heb. 13:8).

Proving Their View of Christ

You might well ask yourself the question, "How do the Jehovah's Witnesses try to prove such a view of Christ?"

First, they may try to prove to you that Michael the archangel was the pre-human existence of Jesus Christ. They will tell you that the name Michael means "who is like God," and they will use the passages in the Bible that refer to Michael, such as Daniel 12:1 where the prince of God's people is called Michael. They will tell you this is really speaking of Jesus in his pre-human state. But all these passages speak only of Michael, the archangel, not of Jesus. Not one of these passages declares the connection between Michael and Jesus which the Jehovah's Witnesses claim. Other passages will be reinterpreted, such as Jude 9,[22] or changed, such as John 8:58 (where "I Am" has been changed to "I have been")[23] in their determination to support their belief in Jesus' pre-earthly existence as an angel.

Second, they may try to disprove the deity of Jesus Christ and lead you to the conclusion that Jesus was only the highest *created* being. To do this they reinterpret certain passages and change others. There are three basic passages they commonly use: John 1:1; Colossians 1:15; Revelation 3:14.

John 1:1: In the *New World Translation of the Christian Greek Scriptures* (their own Bible translation), the latter part of John 1:1 reads, "And the Word was a god" (not "the Word was God" as the Greek translates). John 1:1 actually teaches that Jesus is in essence God. He is a separate person of the Godhead—He was with God, yet He was God. The words of the passage demand this, and even the Jehovah's Witnesses admit this in their literal rendering of the Greek in their *Kingdom Interlinear*. Moreover, the Jehovah's Witnesses' change implies polytheism (belief in more than one God). The following account of a recent discussion with a Jehovah's Witness will illustrate this:[24]

Christian: Do you believe, as is stated in Deuteronomy 6:4, that there is only one God?

Jehovah's Witness: Absolutely!

Christian: In John 1:1 we read, "In the beginning was the Word, and the Word was with God." Who is God in this passage?

Jehovah's Witness: Jehovah.

Christian: And who is the Word?

Jehovah's Witness: Jesus Christ.

Christian: John 1:1 continues to say that "the Word was God." Do you believe that Jesus is God?

Jehovah's Witness: Oh no. He is divine and God-like, but not Jehovah.

Christian: But how can He be divine and not be God?

Jehovah's Witness: He is divine because he is the mighty one. He is not the Almighty God.

Christian: What is He, then?

Jehovah's Witness: He is a god.

Christian: Are you saying that you believe in Jehovah as God and in Jesus as a god?

Jehovah's Witness: Yes! Jesus is *a* god!

Christian: Then you don't believe that Jesus was just an angel while in heaven and only a perfect man on earth. He was at some point a god. Or, are you saying an angel is a god?

Jehovah's Witness: There is only one God!

Christian: Do you believe in a big God and a little god?

Jehovah's Witness: Well, something like that—

Christian: I thought you said you believe in one God?

Jehovah's Witness: I do!

Christian: But $1 + 1 = 2$. A big God and a little god equals two gods. How can that be when, in the very verse you draw your name from, Jehovah says, "Before Me there was no God formed, and there will be none after

70

Me" (Isa. 43:10)? You see, John 1:1 really teaches that Jesus was with God as one of the persons of the Godhead and that He was God.

Colossians 1:15 declares that Jesus Christ is the "first-born of all creation." Twisting the meaning of the term "first-born" to indicate "first created," Jehovah's Witnesses use this passage to prove that Jesus had a beginning. The following discussion between a Jehovah's Witness and a Christian illustrates the difference in use of the term first-born.

Jehovah's Witness: If you turn to Colossians 1:15 you will see that Paul declares Jesus to be the first created being.

Christian: As I read the passage it says that He is the "first-born of all creation," not first created being.

Jehovah's Witness: Well, when a person is born he comes into existence. Thus, first-born means that he was the first one to come into existence.

Christian: But if first-born means the first one to come into existence as you say, how would you interpret Psalm 89:27? "I also shall make him My first-born, the highest of the kings of the earth."

Jehovah's Witness: I don't see what you are getting at.

Christian: First-born here means "the highest of the kings of the earth." Let's check another passage. Turn to Jeremiah 31:9 where it says "and Ephraim is My first-born." Who was born first—Manasseh or Ephraim?

Jehovah's Witness: Manasseh.

Christian: Then why is Ephraim called the first-born?

Jehovah's Witness: What are you getting at?

Christian: The word first-born cannot mean the first one born in this passage, either. In both of these passages it must refer to rank or position of preeminence.

Jehovah's Witness: Oh! I would agree.

Christian: But you see, the term first-born means preeminence regardless of whether it was the first, second or last son. That is the meaning of the term.

71

Jehovah's Witness: What are you getting at?

Christian: Let's go back to Colossians 1:15. Paul is talking about the preeminence of Jesus over all creation in Colossians 1:15, not His being the first creature brought into existence.

Jehovah's Witness: You don't really believe that, do you?

Christian: Paul leaves us in no doubt as to what he means by first-born here. He proceeds to tell us that Jesus is the preeminent one because "in Him all things were created" (Col. 1:16).

Jehovah's Witness: You mean all "other" things.

Christian: No, Paul specifically says "all things."

Jehovah's Witness: Well, Jesus was the first created being who brought all the things, apart from himself, into existence.

Christian: If Paul had meant that Jesus was the first created being, he would have used the specific word for first created, *protoktistos*, not first-born *prototokos*. Furthermore, the passage clearly states that He brought all things into existence. A different word would have been used if he meant all "other" things. He is the preeminent one because He is the creator of all things. "All things have been created . . . for Him" (Col. 1:16). Therefore He must be God. (See Gen. 1:1.)

Jehovah's Witness: But what about Colossians 1:18 where he is "the first-born from the dead"?

Christian: His triumph over death in His resurrection further proves His preeminence over all things, including the power of death.

In Revelation 3:14, Jesus refers to Himself as "the Beginning of the creation of God." Jehovah's Witnesses reinterpret this to mean that Jesus is the beginning of God's creation in the sense that He is the first creation. This passage actually harmonizes with the rest of Scripture, which teaches the deity of Jesus Christ:

Jehovah's Witness: Revelation 3:14 is quite clear about

Jesus being the beginning of things which God created.

Christian: As I read the passage it literally says that He is the "Beginning of the creation of God."

Jehovah's Witness: Same thing!

Christian: Oh no! There is a great difference between being the first one made by God and being the One who made all things—the Creator.

Jehovah's Witness: Agreed!

Christian: It seems to me our difference centers around the word "beginning." That word could easily be translated as origin or source, which would declare Jesus to be the one who begins creation, the origin of creation, the Creator, and then He must be God.

Jehovah's Witness: I agree with you that our difference lies in the translation of the word "beginning." The word means he was the first one made.

Christian: In your own translation of the Bible the same Greek word, *arche*, is translated "origin" in John 1:1. If we carry that translation to Revelation 3:14 it means that Jesus is the origin of the creation of God, or the one who made all things. Can anyone else but God create?

Jehovah's Witness: No

Christian: Then Jesus must be God.

There are other passages that Jehovah's Witnesses will reinterpret in their attempt to demonstrate that Jesus is a created being. They will tell you that Jesus cannot be God because even He Himself said, "The Father is greater than I" (John 14:28). He is a Son and thus different from the Father. Furthermore, Jesus called the Father in heaven His God (see John 17:3). They might even remark, "How can he be the omniscient or all-knowing God when he himself admitted that he did not know the 'day or hour' of His return?" (referring to Mark 13:32. Remember our discussion of these points in chapters 1-4?)

You will face a great challenge in handling the reinterpretation of passages and subtle changes made by the Jeho-

73

History According to the Jehovah's Witnesses

God

God created Michael the angel (pre-human Christ) and through Michael created everything else.

Adam sinned (thus bringing death to all men)

Christ, the perfect man, was born, proved himself faithful, died. Michael, the eternal archangel was recreated and rules in heaven.

Time of the Gentiles

1914   Satan and his demons were banished from heaven and took up residence on earth.
Time of Christ's second (invisible) return

1918   Christ invisibly entered his spiritual temple

1st Resurrection (a spiritual resurrection)	A spiritual resurrection of 144,000 (the anointed class) who will then rule with Christ forever
2nd Resurrection (physical resurrection)	A physical resurrection of the "other sheep" or great crowd—i.e. the Jehovah's Witnesses who were not good enough to be among the 144,-000. They will be ruled by Christ and the 144,000 during the Millennium, will teach others about Christ, and will need to prove themselves faithful to the end (Armageddon).
3rd Resurrection (Resurrection of judgment)	Those who would have been faithful if they had known the truth will be given a chance during the Millennium to hear and accept the truth and prove themselves faithful.
Armageddon	The great last battle when evil and the unfaithful will be totally annihilated. An eternal paradise of the faithful will then be established where Christ and the 144,000 in heaven rule the great crowd in Paradise on earth.

The Millennium is a 1,000-year Judgment Day during which God is separating the faithful from the unfaithful.

Millennium—1,000 years

Paradise

vah's Witnesses. You should be able to answer these. However, do not allow Jehovah's Witnesses to keep you on the defensive. A good offense is the key. Be able to present the true doctrine of the person of Jesus Christ while answering any questions they may have. Focus on the goal of helping them to acknowledge Jesus' lordship—His identity as God and ruler.

Reflecfion

1. Write a summary of the Jehovah's Witness doctrine of Jesus Christ. In what areas is their Jesus different from the Jesus of the Bible?
2. Why should you care if a Jehovah's Witness believes in a different Jesus?

Projects and Proofs

Make a list of passages the Jehovah's Witnesses might use to try to get you to deny the deity of Jesus Christ. Look up each passage and write a response to the Jehovah's Witness interpretation. (Be sure to use materials found in the first section of this book, as well as in other sources.)

Thinking Ahead

Suppose your neighbor is an ardent Jehovah's Witness. One day while you are visiting his house he asks you if you believe that God is a Trinity. How would you respond? What Scripture would you show him from the Bible to explain that God is triune?

Notes

1. Charles Taze Russell, *Studies in the Scripture*, 1st ser., p. 179.
2. *You May Survive Armageddon into God's New World* (1955), p. 112.
3. *Let God Be True*, pp. 39,71 and *The Kingdom Is at Hand* (1944), p. 49.
4. *Your Will Be Done on Earth* (1958), pp. 316, 317; cf. *You May Survive*

Armageddon into God's New World, p. 112.

5. *The Kingdom Is at Hand*, pp. 46, 47.

6. *New Heavens and a New Earth*, p. 24.

7. *The Truth Shall Make You Free* (1943), p. 49.

8. *Let God Be True*, p. 33.

9. *The Kingdom Is at Hand*, p. 49.

10. *Ibid.*

11. J.F. Rutherford, *The Harp of God* (1927), p. 101.

12. *What Has Religion Done for Mankind?* (1951), p. 231.

13. *The Truth Shall Make You Free*, p. 246.

14. *Let God Be True*, p. 40 and *The Kingdom Is at Hand*, pp. 256,259.

15. Russell, *op. cit.*, 5th ser. (1906), p. 454.

16. *Let Your Name Be Sanctified* (1961), p. 272.

17. *Your Will Be Done on Earth*, pp. 316,317.

18. *Let God Be True*, p. 40.

19. *Let Your Name Be Sanctified*, pp. 272, 273.

20. *The Kingdom Is at Hand*, p. 262.

21. Anthony A. Hoekema, *The Four Major Cults* (Grand Rapids: Wm. B. Eerdmans Publishing Co., 1963), pp. 275, 276.

22. This passage was not speaking about Jesus at all, only Michael. If you wish to respond further, you could simply point out that in their theology, Michael originally created Satan (see *The Truth Shall Make You Free*, p. 49). Therefore, Michael was superior to him, as every creator is to his creation. But how can this be when Jude says he had no authority over the one he created? The answer lies in the fact that Michael was only an angel as Satan was and not the agency of creation as the Jehovah's Witnesses claim. Therefore because both were angelic beings and nothing more, Michael had no authority over Satan, but said, "The Lord (referring to Jesus) rebuke you." Interestingly, Michael did not have the authority to rebuke Satan, but Jesus did (see Matt. 4:10). How, then, can Jesus be Michael?

23. In the Greek, *ego eimi* is present active indicative, and thus must be translated "I Am."

24. The material used in these dialogues is from taped interviews between Jehovah's Witnesses and students of Northeastern Bible College.

7

WHAT DO THEY SAY ABOUT GOD?

In talking with Jehovah's Witnesses about God, as a biblical Christian you might at first think that you have the same ideas about God. According to the Jehovah's Witnesses, Jehovah is a God of justice, power wisdom and love; He shows these four eternal attributes at various times and in different ways. His justice demands punishment for breaking His law; His power has been demonstrated on different occasions, such as the flood in Noah's day; His wisdom is revealed in His knowing the future; and His love was manifested in sending Jesus.[1]

Jehovah's Witnesses believe that God is a Spirit Being.[2] He has always existed and will always exist. He is all-knowing and all-powerful, the creator of all things. He exercises His sovereignty over the universe and He alone is entitled to receive worship from His creatures. God is personally known by His name as redeemer—Jehovah.[3]

Jehovah's Witnesses claim to believe in one God, and so do Christians. However, there is a difference here. While the Bible talks about one God who exists in three persons

77

(the Father, Son, and Holy Spirit), Jehovah's Witnesses claim that Jesus is not God (as we saw in the last chapter).

Not only is Jesus rejected as being God, but the Holy Spirit is rejected as the third Person of the God head. According to Jehovah's Witnesses, the Holy Spirit is nothing more than God's invisible, active force[4] working in the lives of His servants to enable them to do His will. The Holy Spirit is impersonal—an it.[5] Therefore, in their translation of the Bible, Jehovah's Witnesses never capitalize the word "spirit" when it refers to the Holy Spirit. They also refer to the Holy Spirit as "it" rather than "he." As far as they are concerned, the Holy Spirit is not God[6] and therefore cannot be equated with Jehovah.

The Trinity Rejected

When Jehovah's Witnesses reject the doctrine of the Trinity, they point out that the word Trinity is not found in the Bible, nor was it used by Jesus and his disciples.

Furthermore, they claim that such a doctrine is most confusing[7] and an insult to "God-given intelligence and reason."[8] Since God is not "a God of confusion" (see 1 Cor. 14:33), they reason that He cannot be the author of such a confusing doctrine. Therefore Satan must be the author of the doctrine of the Trinity.[9] Jehovah's Witnesses believe that this doctrine is one of Satan's most successful attempts at misleading people and keeping them from following the true God, Jehovah.[10]

Where did the doctrine of the Trinity originate? Jehovah's Witnesses claim that this doctrine can be traced back to pagan origins in Babylon, Egypt, etc., long before it was brought into the churches.[11] They believe that biblical teachings about the one true God were corrupted in the fourth century A.D. as a result of a compromise by the churches between their monotheism (belief in one God) and the polytheism (belief in many gods) of the pagan religions at that time. Thus Jehovah's Witnesses express

78

the doctrine of the Trinity as "three Gods in one."[12] By this they mean three gods (polytheism) in one (monotheism), not one God who exists in three persons—the biblical view.

The Trinity Misconceived

When Jehovah's Witnesses rephrase the biblical teaching about the Trinity, they show that they misunderstand the concept of the Trinity.

First of all, while it is true that the word Trinity does not appear in the Bible and was not used by Jesus and His disciples, this in itself does not mean the idea is false. (If it did, the Jehovah's Witnesses themselves would have to abandon several favorite terms on the same basis, such as "theocracy.") The real test is whether or not what the word Trinity defines or describes is in accord with the Bible.

The word Trinity is comprised of two Latin words, *tri* (three) and *unus* (one) and means three-in-one or tri-unity. As we have seen earlier, the early church chose this term as a description of the doctrine of God found in the Bible: one eternal God—the Father, the Son who is Jesus, and the Holy Spirit. Because it describes a biblical reality it is a valid term.

Second, the truth or falsity of the Trinity does not depend upon whether it is reasonable. There are many things that we cannot fully comprehend, and certainly a total understanding of God is beyond our limited human capacities. He alone is God. The truth or falsity of the doctrine of the Trinity depends on what the Bible sets forth. In the Bible God has revealed Himself to us as one true God consisting of three persons—the Father, Son, and Holy Spirit.

Third, the Jehovah's Witnesses state the doctrine of the Trinity incorrectly in their criticism of it. The doctrine of the Trinity does not teach that there are "three gods in one," any more than it teaches that the "Trinity was in Jesus," or that "God is a three-headed God," as many

Jehovah's Witnesses have stated. While it is true that each individual member of the Godhead is properly called God, all three together are called God also; there are not three Gods, but one eternal God consisting of three persons, each of whom is God.

Fourth, Jehovah's Witnesses degrade the doctrine of the Trinity simply because pagan religions had trinitarian deities. Even if this is true, is this sufficient reason to reject the Trinity? If so, we should reject worship, prayer and a host of other practices because pagans worship, pray, etc.

Jehovah's Witnesses have two other misconceptions that make it difficult for them to believe in the Trinity. Since they try to reason out and reduce God to terms man can fully understand, they have difficulty even beginning to understand the triune God. They might reason in this manner: "I am one person. I am a father. I am also a son, and a brother. I am one person existing as father, son and brother. I am all of these at one time. Is that what you mean by the Trinity?" The answer is no! The problem here is the constant attempt by Jehovah's Witnesses to express the infinite tri-personal (three persons) God in terms of finite uni-personal (one person) man. Jehovah's Witnesses want to express God in terms of man and it just cannot be done. He is God. We accept Him as God in three persons because He has revealed Himself that way in the Bible.

Jehovah's Witnesses have trouble believing Jesus is God. Since they define death in terms of total annihilation or cessation of consciousness, they have difficulty reconciling Jesus' death with His deity.[13] Believing that Jesus ceased to exist at death, they want to know, if Jesus is God, "Who ran the universe during the three days that Jesus was dead and in the grave? ... If Jesus was God, then during Jesus' death God was dead and in the grave."[14] The biblical response would be that God (Father, Son and Holy Spirit) did. In the Bible death does not mean annihilation. The physical body dies but the immaterial nature continues to exist. Though Jesus' body died, He continued to exist, and the triune God continued to rule the universe.

The Trinity Disproved?

We have looked at several ways the Jehovah's Witnesses attempt to disprove the doctrine of the Trinity. One way is the attempt to disprove the deity of Jesus Christ and thus destroy the doctrine of the Trinity from that angle.

Another technique is to characterize the doctrine of the Trinity as illogical and confusing and thus label it an undesirable doctrine which must be rejected.

Jehovah's Witnesses also attack certain Bible passages which they believe are weak defenses of the Trinity. Here they choose just certain passages for their purposes and ignore others. One of these is 1 John 5:7 *(KJV)*, "For there are three that bear record in heaven, the Father, the Word, and the Holy Ghost: and these three are one." The Jehovah's Witnesses point out that this passage is not in the oldest manuscripts that we have of the New Testament and, therefore, must be a later addition. They believe that by removing this passage they have destroyed the main support for the Trinity.[15]

While there is a disagreement among the texts regarding 1 John 5:7 (and there are very few of these in the New Testament), 1 John 5:7 is only one passage among many and is only a drop in the bucket, so to speak, of the evidence in the Bible for the Trinity, as we saw in chapter 1.

You will face strong opposition to the doctrine of the Trinity when you speak with Jehovah's Witnesses. Their opposition comes from their misunderstandings about the Trinity and from their insistence on human reason as the basis for truth. Keep in mind that the test of truth is "what does the Scripture say?" (Rom. 4:3).

Encourage Jehovah's Witnesses to lay aside all their literature and to study the Bible alone. Ask them to pray sincerely to God that He will reveal His truth.

Then proceed to support the doctrine of the Trinity to them as it is explained in chapter 1 of this book. Start with the fact that the Bible teaches there is only one true God. They will agree with you. Then tell them that the Father is presented in the Bible as that one true God. Again they will agree with you. Now tell them that the Bible also presents Jesus Christ as that one true God. You will have to demonstrate this to them from the Bible (see chapter 1 of this book). And finally, the Bible presents the Holy Spirit as that one true God. Three persons—one God. Thus the Bible teaches that the true God exists as three persons: the Father, the Son who is Jesus, and the Holy Spirit. To worship any other god or to think of God as less than triune is to reject the God of the Bible.

Reflection

1. What difference does it make whether a person believes in and worships a single-person God or a triune God? Why?
2. Picture a discussion between you and a Jehovah's Witness on the doctrine of the Trinity. What direction would the discussion take? Would you be able to support the concept of the Trinity?

Projects and Proofs

1. There are many passages in the Bible which demonstrate that God is one—the Father is God, Jesus is God, and the Holy Spirit is God. Make a list of 10 passages for each of these concepts, passages that you could explain and use.
2. Write a letter, as you would to one of your friends, explaining the doctrine of the Trinity. Be sure to support your statements with biblical references.

Thinking Ahead

You invited a young Jehovah's Witness to church and

she came. At the end of the service she is appalled at the invitation given to accept Jesus as Saviour. She says to you, "No one is saved by just believing in Jesus." What would you tell her? What passages would you use to show her that salvation is by faith in Jesus Christ alone?

Notes

1. J. F. Rutherford, *The Harp of God*, p. 14
2. *Let God Be True*, pp. 25, 26
3. Ibid, 23
4. *Let God Be True*, p. 108.
5. *Let Your Name Be Sanctified*, p. 269. In contrast to the Jehovah's Witnesses, the Bible describes the Holy Spirit as a person: (1) a masculine pronoun is continually used of Him and even the Jehovah's Witnesses' own translation of the Bible has the masculine pronoun "he" in reference to the Holy Spirit in John 26; (2) the person of the Holy Spirit is affected by the acts of others—He can be resisted (Acts 7:51), grieved (Eph. 4:30); lied to (Acts 5:3) and blasphemed (Matt. 12:31,32); (3) the Holy Spirit performs acts which only a person can do—He wills (1 Cor. 12:11), speaks (Acts 21:11), calls and commissions men (Acts 13:2), teaches (Luke 12:12), thinks and makes decisions (Acts 15:28), and makes intercession (Rom. 8:26,27).
6. *Let God Be True*, pp. 107-111. In contrast to the Jehovah's Witnesses, the Bible describes the Holy Spirit as a divine Person: (1) to lie to the Holy Spirit is to lie to God (Acts 5:3,4); (2) to blaspheme against the Holy Spirit is greater than to blaspheme against the Father or the Son—it is unforgivable (Matt. 12:31,32. In the Jehovah's Witnesses' understanding, how could blasphemy against God's active force be greater than against God Himself?); (3) the Holy Spirit possesses divine attributes—He is all-powerful (Luke 1:35-37), all-knowing (1 Cor. 2:10,11), and eternal (Heb. 9:14); (4) the Holy Spirit performs divine works. He is involved in creation (Gen. 1:2; Job 33:4), the new birth (John 3:5,8), the resurrection of Jesus (Rom. 8:11), and the inspiration of the Scriptures (2 Pet. 1:21). Therefore He is God and the third Person of the Godhead.
7. *"The Word" Who Is He? According to John*, p. 7.
8. *The Truth Shall Make You Free*, p. 45.
9. *Let God Be True*, p. 101.
10. *Ibid*, p. 111.
11. *The Truth Shall Make You Free*, p. 29.
12. *Let God Be True*, p. 100.
13. See "Is There a Trinity?", *Ibid*, pp. 100-111.
14. *Ibid*, p. 109.
15. *What Has Religion Done for Mankind?*, p. 272,273.

8

WHAT DO THEY SAY ABOUT SALVATION?

Why does it matter if a Jehovah's Witness misunderstands Christ or God or the Trinity? The question is similar to, "Why does it matter whether a bill is counterfeit?" Anyone who has tried to spend a counterfeit bill will tell you, "It doesn't work!" It sets up false expectations that cannot be fulfilled. Likewise, in the marketplace of eternity, no one can "spend" a counterfeit faith. It matters to God if a Jehovah's Witness misunderstands Christ or God or the Trinity. Why? Because a wrong understanding of who Jesus is does negate one's understanding of salvation.

"Sirs, what must I do to be saved?" was the question the Philippian jailer asked the apostle Paul (see Acts 16:30). The answer to that question is in verse 31: "Believe in the Lord Jesus, and you shall be saved." This response has been at the heart of the gospel message throughout the history of Christianity.

But what answer will the Jehovah's Witnesses give to this most crucial question? What does the word salvation mean to the Jehovah's Witnesses?

What Jesus Did

According to the Jehovah's Witnesses, the primary purpose of Jesus' being here on earth was not to die for our sins. His primary purpose was to vindicate (provide a defense for Jehovah's name) and establish Jehovah's kingdom.

According to Jehovah's Witnesses, after Adam disobeyed God, Satan challenged God to put a creature on earth who could experience all the temptations Satan could give and still remain faithful to God until death.[1] Faced with such a challenge, God had to vindicate His name before all of His creatures. The burden fell upon His first created being, His son, Michael the archangel. God's son came to earth as Jesus and met all the temptations of Satan, according to the Jehovah's Witnesses. Moreover, he remained true to God until death. In so doing he was able to establish God's kingdom. Thus Jesus was Jehovah's chief witness.

Jehovah's Witnesses claim Jesus also had a secondary purpose in being here. He came to sacrifice his human body as a ransom to God for Adam's sin.[2] Adam's fall had brought about the loss of human perfection. Man became separated from God, sinful, and in bondage to Satan. According to the Jehovah's Witnesses, a perfect human and nothing more than a perfect human was needed to redeem man—i.e., make it possible for mankind to be saved.[3] Since mankind had been separated from God by sin, no one could provide the possibility of salvation except Jesus, he was humanly perfect, a kind of second sinless Adam, so he was the only one who could offer the sacrifice of a perfect body necessary for redemption. He did this at Calvary. Later he appeared in heaven as a glorified high priest presenting his

85

redemptive price to God[4]—his perfect body as a ransom for Adam's sin.

Jehovah's Witnesses believe that Jesus' death removed the effects of Adam's sin, but not the effects of our individual sin. The complete removal of sin will not occur until after Armageddon, when the survivors return to Jehovah and willingly become subject to Him. Then the perfection of the earth will finally become a reality.

Therefore, according to Jehovah's Witnesses, Jesus accomplished both purposes for his coming here to earth. He vindicated God's name by remaining faithful until death through the worst of temptations and, because of his perfection, the sacrifice of his perfect humanity in Adam's place provided a ransom for mankind which would eventually undo all that Adam's sin has done.

What Man Must Do

According to the Jehovah's Witnesses, how does all Jesus accomplished, apply to us individually? How does it affect our relationship with God?

Jehovah's Witnesses teach that the path to the heavenly life involves more than just believing in the Lord Jesus and accepting by faith what Jesus has accomplished. It involves more than accepting and believing the message of God's kingdom. In short, what Jesus accomplished for us as individuals is not enough to restore our relationship with God. Furthermore, Jehovah's Witnesses teach that salvation involves a number of steps, some of which are taken by God and others by man.[5] A person must proclaim the kingdom to show that he believes it.[6] A person must remain loyal to Jehovah throughout this lifetime and the millennium. At the end of the 1,000-year period of the kingdom each person will be "recreated" by God and tested again by Satan. Only those who remain loyal will be granted eternal life[7] at that time.

Actually there are two groups of people who will be

"saved." The first is the "anointed class" or 144,000. These are Jehovah's Witnesses who have been selected by Jehovah on the basis of their worthiness in serving Jehovah continuously. They must carry out their dedication to Jehovah even to death.[8] These are the only ones who are "born again,"[9] according to the Jehovah's Witnesses, and are destined to spend eternity in heaven.[10]

The second group is called the "other sheep" or "great crowd." These are people who will be saved after Armageddon if they pass all the millennial tests. There is no need for these to be "born again."[11] They will be here in paradise on earth,[12] and the "anointed class" will rule over them[13] from heaven.

Jehovah's Witnesses also teach that water baptism is important but that it is not essential to one's salvation. They claim that it is only a symbol of the dedication of one's entire life to the will of Jehovah and identifies one as His minister.

In summary then, Jehovah's Witnesses claim that salvation is of grace and that all credit for salvation belongs to Jehovah.[14] However, salvation is not by faith in Jesus Christ alone. His death merely removed the effects of Adam's sin and made it possible for each of us to work for our salvation. It is our own worthiness—what we have done and how faithful and obedient we have been—that will prove us righteous before God.

Points to Remember

When talking with Jehovah's Witnesses, keep in mind that they believe Jesus' death was nothing more than a perfect man's sacrifice of his body. According to them, God was not "in Christ reconciling the world to Himself" (2 Cor. 5:19). This is clear in an actual dialogue between a Jehovah's Witness and a Christian on this subject:[15]

Jehovah's Witness: I can't buy the idea that Jesus is God. He was only a man.

87

Christian: Do you mean that the passages I have just shown you do not teach that Jesus is God?

Jehovah's Witness: The reason I can't believe that Jesus is God is that his ransom for us wouldn't be fair.

Christian: How is that?

Jehovah's Witness: Satan tempted Adam and Adam sinned. Adam was a man. If Jesus was God, his temptation and his death wouldn't be on an equal basis with Adam's. God for man is not fair.

Christian: Jesus Christ was both man and God. His being a man allowed Him to pay the price for our sins, taking our sins upon Him and dying. But His being God meant that His sacrifice was a perfect one that could extend to all time and to all people. Only God Himself could accomplish this. Jesus was the God-Man.

Keep in mind also that Jehovah's Witnesses believe that Jesus' death was the ransom for what Adam caused. Thus for them, "the blood of Jesus His Son" *does not* cleanse us "from all sin" (1 John 1:7)—only from Adam's sin.

Furthermore, keep in mind that Jehovah's Witnesses believe that they are finally saved by their own worthiness— by being obedient to the Watchtower Society, studying, using Watchtower materials, attending meetings, publishing or giving out Watchtower literature, door-to-door witnessing, etc. Thus for them salvation is not "through faith in Christ" (Gal. 2:16), but by works, even though the apostle Paul clearly states that salvation is "not of yourselves . . . not as a result of works, that no one should boast" (Eph. 2:8,9).

Finally, keep in mind that Jehovah's Witnesses believe that they have not yet received eternal life, because the final test at the end of the 1,000 years is still in the future. Thus, they must deny the words of the apostle John who said, "These things I have written to *you who believe* in the name of the Son of God, in order that you *may know that you have eternal life*" (1 John 5:13, italics added).

"THERE IS ONE GOD"
1 CORINTHIANS 8:6

GOD IS . . .	YAHWEH IS JESUS	JESUS IS . . .
Genesis 1:1		John 1:1-3
Job 33:4	CREATOR	Colossians 1:12-17
Isaiah 40:28		Hebrews 1:8-12
Isaiah 41;4	FIRST	Revelation 1:17
Isaiah 44:6	&	Revelation 2:8
Isaiah 48:12	LAST	Revelation 22:13
Exodus 3:13,14	I AM	John 8:24,58
Deuteronomy 32:39	(EGO EIMI)	John 13:19
Isaiah 43:10		John 18:5
Genesis 18:25		2 Timothy 4:1
Psalm 96:13	JUDGE	2 Corinthians 5:10
Joel 3:12		Romans 14:10-12
Psalm 47		Matthew 2:1-6
Isaiah 44:6-8	KING	John 19:21
Jeremiah 10:10		1 Timothy 6:13-16
Psalm 27:1	LIGHT	John 1:9
Isaiah 60:20		John 8:12
Psalm 106:21		John 4:42
Isaiah 43:3,11	SAVIOUR	Acts 4:10-12
Isaiah 45:21-23		1 John 4:14
Psalm 23		John 10:11
Psalm 100:3	SHEPHERD	Hebrews 13:20
Isaiah 40:11		1 Peter 5:4

Based on a chart developed by William I. Cetnar

In response to the Philippian jailer's question, "What must I do to be saved?" Jehovah's Witnesses respond, "Be obedient to God's organization today (the Watchtower) and work faithfully for Jehovah to the very end if you wish to be saved."

Reflection

1. What do Jehovah's Witnesses believe was the primary purpose of Jesus' coming to earth? Does their belief differ from what the Bible says, and if so, how?
2. What do you believe was Jesus' primary purpose for coming to earth (see John 3:16; 20:31; Rom. 5:6-11; 1 Tim. 1:15)?
3. Write a summary of how one is saved according to the Jehovah's Witnesses. In what areas is their view different from the Bible?

Projects and Proofs

Write a letter that could be sent to any Jehovah's Witness. In it, emphasize that while you know the person is sincere in his/her concept of salvation, you want the person to know the biblical view of salvation because you care about him/her. Use key Bible passages to explain that salvation is by faith in Christ alone, and that any other notion about salvation is a counterfeit. Make it clear that you are acting in love and concern, not judgment.

Thinking Ahead

Suppose someone is setting up a debate. He knows a Jehovah's Witness and decides to place you against the Jehovah's Witness debating whether or not Jesus rose from the dead as a spirit. What Scripture passages would you use to disprove the claim that Jesus was only resurrected as a spirit?

What would you use to prove that Jesus rose bodily from the dead?

Notes

1. *New Heavens and a New Earth*, pp. 147,148,
2. *What Has Religion Done for Mankind?*, pp. 240-245.
3. *Things in Which It Is Impossible for God to Lie* (1965), p. 232.
4. See "A Ransom in Exchange for Many," *Let God Be True*, pp. 112-121.
5. *Aid to Bible Understanding* (1971), p. 735.
6. *From Paradise Lost to Paradise Regained* (1958), p. 249, and *Life Everlasting in Freedom of the Sons of God* (1966), p. 400.
7. *The Truth That Leads to Eternal Life* (1968), pp. 110-113.
8. *Let God Be True*, p. 301.
9. *The Watchtower* (November 15, 1954), p. 681.
10. *Let God Be True*, pp. 297-303.
11. *The Watchtower* (November 15, 1954), p. 681.
12. *The Truth That Leads to Eternal Life*, pp. 102-113.
13. *Ibid.*
14. *Make Sure of All Things*, p. 332.
15. The material used in this dialogue is from taped interviews between Jehovah's Witnesses and students of Northeastern Bible College.

9

WHAT IS
RE-CREATION?

The resurrection of Jesus Christ from the dead is the cornerstone of the Christian faith. At the very center of the gospel message is the fact that "He was raised on the third day according to the Scriptures" (1 Cor. 15:4). This fact is so important that the apostle Paul stated, "If Christ has not been raised, your faith is worthless; you are still in your sins" (1 Cor. 15:17). Furthermore, accepting and believing in Jesus' resurrection is essential to one's relationship with God, for the Bible declares that only if "you confess with your mouth Jesus as Lord, and believe in your heart that God raised Him from the dead, you shall be saved" (Rom. 10:9).

Jehovah's Witnesses say they believe in the resurrection of Jesus Christ from the dead—it was "no illusion or imagined thing."[1] It is a historical fact that Jesus rose from the dead[2] and the empty tomb he left behind is proof of this fact.[3] In their theology, if Jesus had not been raised from the dead, he would not have been able to remove all the effects of Adam's sin. Death, a result of Adam's sin, would have conquered him. They also teach that if Jesus had not been raised from the dead, mankind could not receive the benefits of his ransom sacrifice. For the Jehovah's Witnesses, then, the resurrection of Jesus is affirmed as being a vital part of the divine plan of salvation.

Jehovah's Witnesses do say that Jesus was raised from the grave and that his grave remains empty as a result of this.[4] However, according to them, it was not the body of Jesus that was raised.[5] They are sure that his body was removed from the tomb,[6] but they are not sure what happened to his body. Their literature offers several possibilities: his body could be preserved without decay[7] somewhere as a grand memorial to God's love,[8] or it could have dissolved into gases.[9] Whatever the case, Jehovah's Witnesses are sure of one thing: the *body* of Jesus Christ was not raised from the dead.

What then was raised, according to Jehovah's Witnesses? If it was not the material part of Jesus that was raised, perhaps it was his immaterial nature—his soul and/or his spirit. According to the Jehovah's Witnesses, the soul and the body are the same thing.[10] So, if his body did not rise, his soul did not rise from the dead. Furthermore, the Jehovah's Witnesses believe that the spirit is nothing more than breath.[11] In dying Jesus gave up this spirit or breathed his last breath, and thus his spirit could not be raised from the dead.

If it was not the body of Jesus nor his soul nor his spirit that was raised from the dead, what then was resurrected according to Jehovah's Witnesses? In actuality it was nothing. It was not Jesus who rose from the dead. Though Jehovah's Witnesses affirm belief in the resurrection of Jesus Christ, they do not really believe in his resurrection.

Jehovah's Witnesses believe in re-creation. They believe that Jehovah remembers your life pattern and then creates you again, or re-creates you after death as He remembers you.[12] In Jesus' case, Jehovah remembered the pre-human existence of Jesus as an angel, and thus re-created the angel Michael, the archangel, only this time immortal and of a divine order.[13]

Following His re-creation, the angel manifested many bodies during the 40 days he was on earth. According to the Jehovah's Witnesses, he even assumed a body like that in which Jesus was crucified, with nail prints in his hands and feet, to convince his disciples that it was the same Jesus (when it really wasn't).[14]

His re-creation is the guarantee that all who die will be re-created one day as Jehovah remembers them at the end of the 1,000-year reign called the millennium. During that time there will be teachers of his Law who will instruct the unlearned and unjust in the ways of Jehovah.[15] These will all be given a chance to accept Jehovah, after which Jehovah will prove their sincerity by allowing Satan to test them for a time. Those who remain faithful will live on earth forever; those who fail will face annihilation (complete extinction).[16]

Proving Re-Creation?

How do Jehovah's Witnesses attempt to prove their doctrine of re-creation? First of all, they assume that resurrection is re-creation. They use the term resurrection continuously. But since they believe that nothing regarding Jesus is raised from the dead, it cannot be resurrection.

Second, they lift certain passages out of context to prove their doctrine. A favorite is 1 Corinthians 15:50: "Now I say this, brethren, that flesh and blood cannot inherit the kingdom of God." Jehovah's Witnesses claim that since a body is "flesh and blood" it "cannot inherit the kingdom of God." However, the passage actually indicates that the way we are now— flesh and blood—will not inherit the kingdom. The next verse indicates why—there must be a change. This corruptible, mortal body must become incorruptible and immortal (see 1 Cor. 15:53,54) at the return of Jesus Christ to this earth (see 1 John 3:2,3). Then it is capable of inheriting the kingdom of God.

Third, they reinterpret certain passages to prove that Jesus rose as a spirit, and thus conclude that he must have been recreated. They often use 1 Peter 3:18, in which Peter states that Jesus was "put to death in the flesh, but made alive in the spirit." Jehovah's Witnesses claim this teaches that Jesus was resurrected as a spirit. Actually, a better translation would be "made alive by the spirit," teaching that Jesus was raised from the dead by the Holy Spirit (cf. Rom. 8:11).

Fourth, they use the passages in which Jesus was not recognized by people who saw Him after His resurrection, Jehovah's Witnesses thus argue that it could not have been Jesus who rose bodily from the dead but a spirit who, on occasion, manifested a human body for specific reasons.[17]

Three passages frequently used are John 20:11ff; 21:4ff and Luke 24:13ff. However, in context, each of these actually poses no problem to belief in the resurrection of Jesus Christ from the dead.

John 20:11-17: In verse 14 John records that Mary "turned around, and beheld Jesus standing there, and did not know that it was Jesus." In fact, she even thought He was the gardener (see John 20:15). Certainly it is understandable that Mary did not recognize Jesus immediately. She was still shaken and grieved by His death. Besides that, it was still dark outside when this took place. But, as soon as Jesus said, "Mary," she knew at once that it was He (see John 20:16).

John 21:4-12: In verse 4 we read that "Jesus stood on the beach; yet the disciples did not know that it was Jesus." Here it was early in the morning. The disciples had fished all night. They were a distance from the shore and were not expecting Jesus to be there. However, John did recognize Him (see John 21:7).

Luke 24:13-31: Here two disciples were walking on the

road to Emmaus. Jesus was walking with them, but they did not recognize Him. Verse 16 tells why: "But their eyes were prevented from recognizing Him." After Jesus had accomplished His purpose in teaching them, then "their eyes were opened and they recognized Him" (Luke 24:31). Jesus was not in another form as a spirit, but there physically before them. However, their eyes were kept from recognizing Him until the right moment.

In talking with Jehovah's Witnesses, keep in mind the difference between resurrection and re-creation. Every case of resurrection from the dead mentioned in the Bible records, without exception, a bodily resurrection of the same person who died. For example, there can be no doubt that it was Lazarus' body that was raised, observable to all, and that it was Lazarus himself who was present (see John 11:43-47; 12:1-11).

Remember that Jesus Christ said, when speaking of His own death and resurrection, "Destroy this temple, and in three days I will raise it up" (John 2:19). The apostle John comments that "He was speaking of the temple of His body. When, therefore, He was raised from the dead, His disciples remembered that He said this; and they believed the Scripture, and the word which Jesus had spoken" (John 2:21,22).

When you talk about Jesus' resurrection with someone who believes in His re-creation as an immortal spirit, point to the words the risen Lord Jesus Himself spoke to the disciples, which stand in marked contrast: "See My hands and My feet, that it is I Myself; touch Me and see, for a spirit does not have flesh and bones as you see that I have" (Luke 24:39).

Reflection

1. What is the difference between what the Jehovah's Witnesses believe about resurrection and what the Bible says?

2. Does it make any difference whether or not one believes in the resurrection of Jesus Christ from the dead? In His bodily resurrection? Why?

Projects and Proofs

Write a response that could be used with Jehovah's Witnesses to teach them the true doctrine of resurrection as contrasted with re-creation.

Notes

1. *Let God Be True*, p. 273.
2. *Ibid*, p. 274.
3. *Awake!* (June 8, 1955), p. 26.
4. *Ibid*, cf. *The Truth Shall Make You Free*, p. 263. Jehovah's Witnesses even teach that the religious leaders of His day tried to "thwart the Son of God's coming forth from the grave" (*Let God Be True*, pp. 273,274).
5. *The Truth Shall Make You Free*, p. 264.
6. Rutherford, *op. cit.*, p. 170.
7. *Ibid*.
8. Russell, *op. cit.*, 2nd ser. (1907), p. 129.
9. *Ibid*.
10. See "What Is Man?" *Let God Be True*, pp. 66-75; cf. *Make Sure of All Things*, p. 349.
11. *Make Sure of All Things*, p. 357 ff.
12. *Ibid*, p. 311.
13. *Let God Be True*, pp. 40,41 and *Your Will Be Done on Earth*, pp. 316,317.
14. *The Kingdom Is at Hand*, pp. 256-259.
15. *Let God Be True*, p. 270.
16. *The Kingdom Is at Hand*, pp. 364,365.
17. Russell, *op. cit.* pp. 127,128

SECTION III

MORMONS AT YOUR DOOR

The person and work of Jesus Christ according to the Mormons

10

MEET THE
MORMONS

Mormonism traces its lineage back to Jesus Christ Himself, and beyond that to the true Jewish (Old Testament) religion. Within this history, Mormonism claims that churches had been existing outside the "true" faith for centuries until Joseph Smith, Jr., whom Mormons revere as a prophet of God, restored the one true church of Christ. Mormonism claims to be that one true church.

Joseph Smith, Jr. was born on December 23, 1805 in Sharon, Vermont. When he was about 10, his family moved to Palmyra, New York, and shortly thereafter to Manchester, located between Palmyra and Canandaigua, in New York State.

According to Mormonism,[1] there was much religious activity in Palmyra in those days, with revivalist after revivalist visiting the area. Religious groups and churches were looking for members. Joseph's mother, brothers and sisters joined the Presbyterian church; he was somewhat inclined toward the Methodist church. However, he found himself confused. Which one was right? Which one represented the true church? So, in 1820, claiming the promise of James 1:5, he went into the woods to seek God's guidance as to which church he should join.[2] James 1:5 reads, "But if any of you lacks wisdom, let him ask of God, who gives to all men generously and without reproach and it will be given to him." As he began to pray, suddenly a pillar of light began to shine over his head. It is claimed[3] that two persons appeared to him in the light and one said, "This is My Beloved Son. Hear Him!" So Joseph asked this person which of the churches he should join, if any. He was told not to join any of them because their creeds were an abomination (something disgusting) as far as God was concerned.[4] So he returned home.

On September 21, 1823, while Joseph Smith, Jr. was in prayer in his room, the angel Moroni[5] appeared to him and told him of some gold plates. Moroni claimed they contained "the fullness of the gospel" as revealed by Jesus Christ to earlier inhabitants of this continent. Also with the plates were two seer stones, the Urim and Thummim, which would be used in the translation of the plates. (There is debate about whether these seer stones were spectacles or stones viewed within a hat.) The next night the angel appeared again, telling him where the plates were buried. Joseph went to the hill Cumorah and, after removing a large stone, he uncovered a stone box. In the box were the gold plates, a breastplate (armor) and two stones in silver bowls, but the angel prohibited him from taking the plates with him at this time.

Four years later to the day, Joseph Smith, Jr. was allowed to take the plates and begin translation.[6] He moved to his father-in-law's house in Harmony, Pennsylvania, where he was joined by a wealthy farmer, Martin Harris, who became his scribe in the translation process. After 116 pages were translated, Harris took the translation home to his wife, who was very doubtful of Joseph's integrity. At this time the manuscript disappeared from the Martin's house, and God allegedly told Joseph that this portion of the plates would not be translated again. Martin Harris was not allowed to continue the translation process.

Oliver Cowdery, a relative of Joseph, became the new scribe. In April of 1829, while translating the plates, he and Smith learned that the plates taught baptism for the remission (release from guilt) of sins. Joseph had never been baptized. So they went out into the woods to pray about this. On May 15, 1829 John the Baptist appeared to them and ordained them to the Aaronic Priesthood. They then baptized one another. Some time after this, Peter, James and John appeared to them and conferred upon them the Melchizedek Priesthood.[7] Thus there are two priesthoods in Mormonism: Aaronic, referring to Aaron (see Exod. 28), and Melchizedek, which is the highest order of priesthood (see Heb. 5:6; 6:20).

In June, 1829, the work of translating the plates was completed and soon the first edition of the *Book of Mormon* was ready. It should be noted here that the plates are no longer in existence, Joseph Smith having claimed he returned them to the angel Moroni when the translation was complete.

At a formal meeting in the home of Peter Whitmer, Sr., in Fayette,[8] New York on April 6, 1830, the one true church was organized in the state of New York. The Church of Christ (later named the Church of Jesus Christ of Latter-day Saints) came into existence.[9]

Joseph Smith, Jr. and his followers were not accepted or liked in western New York State, so in 1831 they moved about 300 miles west to Kirkland, Ohio. Here they settled and erected a temple. But arguments began to erupt within the church.

After a split in the church and subsequent turmoil, Joseph and his followers left for their colony at Far West, Missouri. Here they met more opposition and persecution, so they turned eastward, crossed the Mississippi and settled, on May 1, 1839, in what was to become Nauvoo, Illinois. They built a flourishing city.

At first things were peaceful, but soon opposition began. One of the reasons was the polygamy (practice of having several wives) being practiced among the Mormon leaders. (At this time, polygamy was a Mormon teaching.) Violence followed. In 1844, four Mormon leaders were jailed in Carthage. On June 27, 1844, a mob rushed the jail and, in a gun battle, Joseph Smith, Jr. was killed.[10]

Now that the Mormons were without their prophet, several claimed to be the next prophet after Smith. Alpheus Cutler had a vision in which he was to become the leader. He was rejected and so he led a group away, founding the Church of Jesus Christ in Northern Iowa and Wisconsin. James Strang also had visions and claimed to have received a letter from Joseph Smith, Jr. appointing Strang lawful successor just 10 days before Joseph was assassinated. Strang was put out of the church and he too founded his own group, the Church of Jesus Christ of Latter-day Saints in Northern Michigan. Sidney Rigdon claimed succession and was rejected. He led a group to Pennsylvania where he founded the Church of Jesus Christ. The Smith family, under the leadership of Emma Smith, first wife of Joseph Smith, Jr., subsequently claimed that the leadership must remain within the family. This group pulled together scattered disciples who had not gone with the other Mormon groups, and founded the reorganized Church of Jesus Christ of Latter-day Saints, headquartered in Independence, Missouri. The main group, under the leadership of Brigham Young, left for the west shortly after, finally settling by the Great Salt Basin in Utah. Here Brigham Young was declared president of the Church of Jesus Christ of Latter-day Saints, headquartered in Salt Lake City, Utah.

For them he was the successor to Joseph Smith, Jr. as the prophet of God.

Mormonism today is one of the most influential counterfeits of Christianity. In talking with Mormons about their beliefs, you will need to remember the following information about the name "Mormon," their view of the Bible, and their test for truth.

The Church of Jesus Christ of Latter-day Saints

Keep in mind that there are several different groups which are called Mormon. There is the Church of Jesus Christ (Cutlerites); the Church of Jesus Christ (Bickertonites); the Church of Christ, Temple Lot; the Reorganized Church of Jesus Christ of Latter-day Saints; the Church of Jesus Christ of Latter- day Saints (Strangites); the Church of Jesus Christ of Latter-day Saints (Brighamites), and others. There have been, perhaps, as many as a 100 offshoots from the original church.[11] These groups all have two things in common: They accept Joseph Smith, Jr. as a prophet of God and the *Book of Mormon* as the Word of God—hence they are called "Mormons." However, each group claims to be the only true church, rejecting all the others as apostates, and each one has some differences in doctrine and practice from the others.

Keep in mind that the material presented in this section is that of the Church of Jesus Christ of Latter-day Saints whose headquarters is in Salt Lake City, Utah. This is the largest group of Mormons and the fifth largest religious group in the United States. If you are talking with someone from any other Mormon group, be sure to learn what his/her doctrines are.

Is the Bible Unreliable?

From the very beginning, Mormons said the Bible is unreliable, even though it is used by them and they lay claim to being biblical. The eighth Article of Faith in Mormonism states, "We believe the Bible to be the word of God as far as it is translated correctly." Mormonism, in reality, needs an unreliable Bible because the Bible contradicts almost all of Mormonism's doctrines and practices. Mormons are taught that the Catholic Church corrupted the texts so that the Bible today cannot always be trusted. This means that when you share your faith with Mormons, whenever a passage from the Bible contradicts their belief, they will think that passage is one of the places in which the text of the Bible has been corrupted.

Remember that you may need to support the Bible's integrity (trustworthiness) before you can continue to show them what the Bible actually does teach. The Dead Sea Scrolls, dated before the time of Jesus and thus before the Catholic Church, are virtually identical to the Old Testament text we use today. There is no corruption there.[12] And the New Testament text with its numerous manuscripts, many of them as early as A.D. 200, shows only minor variations in the text and no large blocks of material missing, as Mormons claim.[13] The fact is that Mormonism ignores modern textual studies which establish the reliability of both the Old and New Testaments texts beyond question. Sometimes, if this is simply stated, the discussion ends.

Be ready, though, to demonstrate the trustworthiness of the text of the Bible when talking with Mormons.

Is Prayer the Test for Truth?

If the Bible is not the basis of Mormonism, what is? From the very beginning Mormonism has been based on a subjective experience—praying about something and having God confirm it to their hearts. This is still the basis of accepting Mormonism today and the test for all truth as far as Mormons are concerned.

A quotation from the *Book of Mormon* is printed in front of most of the missionary editions of the *Book of Mormon*. It says:

"And when ye receive these things, I would exhort you that ye would ask God, the Eternal Father, in the name of Christ, if these things are not true; and if ye shall ask with a sincere heart, with real interest, having faith in Christ, he will manifest the truth of it unto you, by the power of his Holy Ghost, and by the power of the Holy Ghost, ye may know the truth of all things" (Moroni 10:4,5).

The Uniform System for Teaching Families (a handbook for talking to non-Mormon families), which Mormon missionaries currently use, continually stresses "Do you feel . . . " placing emphasis on *feeling* good about religion. The climactic questions which lead up to one's praying about Mormonism, according to Moroni 10:4,5 are as follows:

"If you sincerely asked your Heavenly Father to guide you, do you feel He would deceive you?" (C-28, *The Uniform System for Teaching Families*). "Mr. Brown, do you feel that you can know the truth of these things by pondering them sincerely and by asking the Lord in prayer?" (C-29).

Mormons have prayed about Mormonism, the *Book of Mormon* and the prophet Joseph Smith, Jr. They are always willing to "bear you their testimony" of this. In fact, some will even give Moroni 10:4,5 as the basis for their faith. This is why Mormons, when pressed by evidence and argument, will say, "But I've prayed about it and I know it is true."

Keep in mind that a Mormon essentially *feels* good about his religion. He has subjectively accepted it by praying about it and that is why he is so sure it is true. However, we are not supposed to test truth by prayer and feeling but by what God says in His Word, the Bible. Before praying about something, see if God has not already spoken about it. For example, if a voice told you to rob a bank and give all the money to the poor, you wouldn't have to pray about it. Exodus 20:15 says, "You shall not steal." Praying about something which God has already spoken against is testing God, not testing the truth. This testing invites His wrath and leaves you open to other forces. Newspapers often describe the crimes of people who claim that God told them to do it. Testing God almost cost Balaam his life (see Num. 22:12-33).[14]

If a Mormon brings up James 1:5, point out that this passage does not teach that prayer is the test for all truth. The passage is written to Christians, not to all persons, and the context is a discussion of coping with trials. The test for all truth is God's Word, the Bible. When the Bereans were confronted with the apostle Paul's message, they did not go out to the woods and pray about it until God confirmed it and they felt good about it. They examined "the Scriptures daily, to see whether these things were so" (Acts 17:11). And so must all who would be true to God. The test for truth is not whether one feels good about one's religion, how moral or good it is or how many good works it is inspiring. No one should accept anything as belonging to the only true God that contradicts God's Word.

Reflection

1. Have you ever talked about religion with a Mormon? If so, what was your discussion like? Did you note any differences in beliefs?
2. Have you ever considered the possibility that Mormon teaching might not be biblically Christian?
3. Having read this chapter, what can you expect when talking to Mormons? What would you say to the charge that the Bible is untrustworthy? If a Mormon said, "But I've prayed about it and I know it is true," how would you respond?

Projects and Proofs

Read some material on the authenticity and reliability of

both the Old and New Testament. Such books as F.F. Bruce's *The New Testament Documents: Are They Reliable?* and Josh McDowell's, *Evidence That Demands a Verdict* are excellent sources. Make a list of facts that you could use with a Mormon, if needed, to prove for you that the text of the Bible is reliable.

Thinking Ahead

Here you are on vacation and two young men, neatly dressed, come to visit you to share their faith. They tell you that Jesus was the first-born of many spirit children to a Heavenly Father and Heavenly Mother, and that He became God. Do you think you could respond to this? If so, what passages from the Bible would you use?

Notes

1. Contrary to current Mormon teaching, it has been proven historically that there was no revival between 1819-1824 in Palmyra. Revival did not occur until the fall of 1824. See Wesley P. Walters, *New Light on Mormon Origins* (Utah Christian Tract Society, Box 725, La Mesa, CA, 92041).
2. *Pearl of Great Price*, Joseph Smith 2:10.
3. Contrary to current Mormon teaching, there are differing and contradictory accounts of this first vision given by Joseph Smith, Jr. himself. One claims he was 14 years old at the time, while other accounts say 16 and 17. One claims "two Personages" appeared to him, while other accounts say it was "an angel," "many angels," or "The Lord." *See Dialogue: A Journal of Mormon Thought* (Autumn 1966, vol. 1), pp. 29ff. and *BYU Studies* (Spring 1969), pp. 275ff. for a summary of these different accounts in Mormonism.
4. *Pearl of Great Price*, Joseph Smith 2:-9.
5. Contrary to current Mormon teaching, in the 1851 edition of the *Pearl of Great Price*, the angel's name was Nephi, not Moroni (see page 41; cf. *Millennial Star*, vol. 3, pp. 53,71 and *Times and Seasons*, vol. 3, pp. 749, 753).
6. *Pearl of Great Price*, Joseph Smith 2:59-62.
7. *Ibid.*, 2:72.
8. All the early writings have the church organized at Manchester, but today it is placed at Fayette.
9. *Doctrines and Covenants*, p. 20.
10. See *Documentary History of the Church*, vol. 6, pp. xli, 617,618; vol. 7, pp. 100-103.

11. See Kate Carter, *Denominations That Base Their Beliefs on the Teachings of Joseph Smith, the Mormon Prophet* (published by the Mormons).
12. *E.g.*, Gleason Archer, *A Survey of Old Testament Literature* (Chicago: Moody Press, 1964), p. 19.
13. *E.g.*, F.F. Bruce, *The New Testament Documents: Are They Reliable?* (Downer's Grove, IL: Inter-Varsity Press, 1960), p. 20.
14. Wally Tope, "Maximizing Your Witness to Mormons," *Contemporary Christianity*, vol. 7, no. 3 (September-November 1977), pp. 2-11.

11

JESUS
IS GOD,
BUT...

"Do you believe in Jesus Christ?" is *not* the most important question to ask to find out whether a religion is genuinely Christian. Many would misleadingly answer yes to this question. The first Article of Faith in The Church of Jesus Christ of Latter-day Saints (hereafter called Mormons) states, "We believe . . . in His Son, Jesus Christ." It is on this basis that Mormons refer to themselves as Christians, for they do believe in Jesus Christ. However, the real question which Jesus Christ Himself asked of the Pharisees was, "What do you think about the Christ?" (Matt. 22:42).

What exactly do the Mormons "think about the Christ?" It is the answer to this question that determines whether one belongs to Jesus or not, and whether Mormonism is Christian or not.

Jesus—the Spirit Child

According to the Mormons, Jesus Christ is a created

being. He is the "First born Spirit Child"[1] of a long line of children who were sexually conceived in spirit form by a Heavenly Father, who is the God of this universe, and a Heavenly Mother.[2] In fact, all people—Jesus, Lucifer, we and others who have lived and will live on earth—were first born in a spirit form in heaven. Jesus, being the first-born, is our eldest brother.

In the spirit world Jesus, or Jehovah as He was then known, was the brother of Lucifer. He was chosen by the Heavenly Father to be the Saviour of the world. Lucifer, one of the other sons of God, argued with this decision and offered to go to earth and be the Saviour.[3] Lucifer's idea was to force mankind to be saved. Jesus wanted to allow man to choose, which the Heavenly Father preferred. Lucifer became very angry over this and rebelled against the Father, taking one third of the existing spirits with him. These were cast out from heaven and became Satan and his demons.

Jesus, Child of . . .

Mormons claim that coming from the spirit world, Jesus was born of Mary. He was not conceived by Joseph because Jesus was special to the Heavenly Father. He was not conceived by the Holy Ghost because the Holy Ghost did not have a body. The Holy Ghost is a separate God from the Father. If the Holy Ghost conceived Jesus, then Jesus would not be the only begotten Son of the Father, but rather of the Holy Ghost.[4] Jesus was conceived by the Heavenly Father, a god of flesh and bones, through sexual relations with Mary, an earthly woman. The only difference between Jesus and any other human is that his Heavenly Father (Father God who has a body) was literally his earthly father, who conceived him in the physical world as well.[5]

Because celestial marriage (marriage in the Temple) is one requirement for godhood or exaltation, Jesus had to be married. Thus Mormons believe that while Jesus was on earth he was married, perhaps to Mary, Martha and Mary Magdalene.[6] The Mormon Jesus was not only polygamous, but he even had children by these wives.[7] He died on the cross and rose physically from the dead. He appeared to many during the 40 days after his resurrection and then ascended to heaven. He also appeared in his resurrected body to the early American Indians—the people of the *Book of Mormon*.[8] Jesus Christ is going to return again to this earth one day in physical form to establish his kingdom.

Jesus, Our Prototype

According to the Mormons, Jesus "attained unto godhead" (he became a god)[9] through his consistent effort and absolute obedience to all the gospel truth and Law.[10] He has become our prototype, our model or standard of salvation. What Jesus was, we were—spirits procreated (given birth) by the same parents (Father God and Mother God) in heaven. As Jesus became a god; so male Mormons can become gods through continual effort and obedience.[11] The role of the female is to help the male attain godhood. She cannot attain it herself, but simply "goes along" if her husband becomes a god.

Passages to Consider

How do the Mormons attempt to prove these beliefs about the person of Jesus Christ? Although Mormons like to point to later revelations or other writings which they claim to be Scripture, such as the *Book of Mormon, Doctrines and Covenants* and *Pearl of Great Price*, they do attempt to prove their theology from the Bible itself by reinterpreting biblical passages in the light of their preconceived theology.

Mormons attempt to prove the doctrine that all human beings existed prior to this life in spirit form from such passages as Hebrews 12:9; Jeremiah 1:5 and Romans 9:11, 12.

In Hebrews 12:9 God is referred to as the "Father of spirits." Mormons interpret this to mean that God fathers— gives birth to—spirit children. James 1:17 is quite similar to the Hebrews passage in declaring God to be the "Father of lights." In both of these passages the Bible is saying that God is the creator, not the procreator, of all things, including spirits and lights.

In Jeremiah 1:5 God says, "Before I formed you in the womb I knew you, and before you were born I consecrated you." Of course, Mormons interpret this to mean that God knew Jeremiah in the spirit world. Actually, this passage means that God, being God and knowing all things, even that which will be, knew about Jeremiah and had a purpose for him before he came into existence.

Likewise Romans 9:11,12 does not teach that Esau and Jacob existed in the spirit world before coming here, or that the "older will serve the younger" as a result of what they did in the spirit world. The passage specifically states that their position with God was not because Jacob and Esau had "done anything good or bad," but that "God's purpose according to His choice"—His plan—would be fulfilled in their lives. The Bible simply does not teach that we lived in a spirit existence before coming to this world.

Mormons also attempt to prove that Jesus was one of these spirit-conceived children, and that he was the first spirit child born of the Father and Mother in heaven. They will tell you that Jesus is called the "Son of God," and therefore he must be the spirit child of the Heavenly Father. But, as we have seen in an earlier section, the Bible uses "Son of God" to describe the relationship between the persons of the Godhead, and refers clearly to the deity of Jesus Christ.

Colossians 1:15 is frequently used by the Mormons to prove that Jesus was the first spirit child. In this passage

113

Jesus is referred to as the "first-born of all creation." But all this passage in Colossians states is that Jesus has preeminence or "first right" over all creation because He is the creator of all things that are "in the heavens and on earth . . . all things have been created through Him and for Him" (Col. 1:16).

Finally, Mormons attempt to prove that Jesus is one god among many, and that he has progressed to godhood. In order to become a god, Jesus had to be married. So Mormons have taught that Jesus himself was the bridegroom at the marriage of Cana in Galilee in John 2.[12] However, John records that Jesus was invited to the wedding; therefore, it could not have been His own wedding.

Mormons also point to Isaiah 53:10, which says of the Messiah or Jesus, "He will see His offspring." They believe this is a reference to Jesus on the cross seeing his natural children before he died.[13] The correct interpretation is that "His offspring" in this passage are His spiritual seed—all those who believe in Him and have accepted the benefits of His sacrifice at Calvary. Thus, it is not a reference to any natural children.

Mormonism teaches that Jesus Christ was not a god originally but that he became a god through his obedience and persistence. The Bible clearly teaches that Jesus is and always was God (see John 1:1; Col. 2:9). In Jesus' case it was not man becoming a god, as Mormons believe, but God (the second Person of the Godhead) becoming a man (see John 1:1,14,18; Phil. 2:6-8).

You must keep in mind the fact that Mormons approach the Bible with a preconceived theology, and they interpret passages from the Bible according to it. They do not build their theology from what the Bible, the Word of God, teaches about Jesus. While it will be important for you to show Mormons that the passages they use do not teach what they claim, it will be essential for you to be able to present to them the truth about the person of Jesus Christ.

He is the second Person of the eternal triune God.

He, being God, added to Himself a human nature, being conceived in the womb of the virgin Mary by the Holy Spirit.

He came to die on the cross of Calvary for all our sins and He rose triumphant from the dead. He is coming one day for his own.

He is "our great God and Savior, Christ Jesus" (Titus 2:13).

Reflection

1. Does it make any difference what one believes about Jesus Christ? Why?
2. Summarize what Mormons believe about Jesus Christ. In what areas is their belief about Jesus different from the Bible? If asked, how would you respond to these differences? What passages from the Bible would you use?

Projects and Proofs

On one side of a page, outline the major points of the Mormon teaching on Jesus Christ. On the other side, parallel the Mormon teaching with what the Bible teaches. Look up passages to support what the Bible says, and record them on the paper.

Thinking Ahead

You have heard so much about the Mormon entertainers Donny and Marie Osmond that you decide to see what Mormonism is all about. You call the Mormon church in your area and they send two missionaries to talk to you. They tell you that our God is one of many gods, that He was once a man and that He even had a body of flesh and bones. Would you be able to respond to these ideas about God? If so, what would you say? What passages would you use?

115

Notes

1. Bruce McConkie, *What Mormons Think of Christ*, p. 31.
2. Milton R. Hunter, *Gospel Through the Ages*, p. 98.
3. *Ibid.*, pp. 15,16.
4. Brigham Young, *Journal of Discourses*, vol. 1, pp. 50,51; cf. James Talmage, *The Articles of Faith*, pp. 466,467.
5. Talmage, *op.cit.*, pp. 466,473 and *Journal of Discourses*, vol. 4, pp. 217,218.
6. Orson Pratt, *The Seer*, p. 159 (Washington, D.C. Edition).
7. *Journal of Discourses*, vol. 2, p. 82.
8. *Book of Mormon*, 3 Nephi 11-28.
9. McConkie, *op. cit.*, p. 36.
10. Hunter, *op.cit.*, p. 51.
11. *Ibid.*
12. *Journal of Discourses*, vol. 2, pp. 82,210.
13. *Ibid.*, p. 82.

12

GOD MAY
BE GOD,
BUT...

In the preceding chapter we saw that Mormon teachings say that Jesus originally came into existence in the spirit world through sexual relations between God, the Heavenly Father, and His wife, the Heavenly Mother. He was then born into this physical world through sexual relations between God, the Heavenly Father (remember, he is a glorified man) and Mary, an earthly woman. He progressed to godhood through much effort and obedience and became a god. Therefore there are at least two gods in the Mormon faith—the Heavenly Father and Jesus.

From this it is obvious that Mormon belief is different from the Bible in what it says about God as well as about Jesus. What do Mormons really believe about God?

Is Matter Eternal?

According to Mormonism, matter, not God, is the ultimate substance or essence and is eternal.[1] Intelligences from which man was derived existed within this matter. Thus Mormons speak of the fact that we have always existed as intelligences.[2] Furthermore, when Mormons speak of God creating the earth, they do not mean that He created it out of nothing, for matter is eternal. They mean that He reorganized it from already existing matter. This is the Mormon account of "creation."[3]

Was God Once a Man?

According to Mormonism, man came from these intelligences in matter. Man became god and he gave birth to spirit children. Some of these became gods, giving birth to other spirit children, and so on, indicating a multiplicity of generations in successive worlds.[4]

The Heavenly Father, who is the God of this world, was a spirit child of a previous god. He was then born on another earth and there he had to earn and attain godhood.[5] He could not have become a god without a helpmate and so he was married.[6] He died on this other earth, and was physically resurrected from the dead. Thus he is a god with a body of flesh and bones. He is the Heavenly Father and his wife became the Heavenly Mother[7] according to Mormon teaching.

Can Men Become Gods?

According to Mormonism, "As man is, God once was; as God is, man may be."[8] As the Heavenly Father and Jesus Christ were the results of two births, one in the spirit world and one here, so are we the results of two births. As the Heavenly Father and Jesus Christ attained godhood, so can some of us. The same path is open to all Mormon males to be obedient and fulfill the same requirements and become gods.[9] This idea that the Heavenly Father and Jesus Christ worked their way up from humanity to deity, and that other human beings can do likewise, is known as the doctrine of eternal progression.

How Many Gods Are There?

According to Mormonism there are many gods now and there are many more who will become gods. Orson Pratt once remarked, "If we should take a million of worlds like this and number their particles, we shall find that there are more Gods than there are particles of matter in those worlds."[10]

Thus, when Mormons refer to there being only one God, they mean there is one god with whom this world is involved, the Heavenly Father, for there are many other gods. When they speak of "the Trinity," their first Article of Faith states, "We believe in God the Eternal Father, and in His Son, Jesus Christ and in the Holy Ghost." However, they do not define the Trinity as "three Persons in the one God"; according to Mormonism, there are "three distinct personages and three Gods."[11] The Mormon doctrine of the Trinity consists of the Heavenly Father as one god; Jesus Christ, who became god, as another god; and the Holy Ghost, a spirit child of the Heavenly Father and Heavenly Mother who has not yet received a physical body, as still another god.[12] (Mormons distinguish the Holy Spirit from the Holy Ghost, the Holy Ghost being God's intelligence-gathering network.)

Polytheism?

Mormons will attempt to show you that the Bible supports what they believe. They realize that the Bible does not support all their beliefs, such as the eternal nature of matter. The Bible clearly teaches that God created the world (see John 1:3; Col. 1:16,17; and Heb. 1:1-3). They realize that the Bible does not even mention the idea of a Heavenly Mother. They generally point to those areas in which they can reinterpret passages to support their preconceived theology.

Mormons will attempt to use the Bible to prove the existence of many gods (polytheism). They refer to *Elohim*, an

Old Testament name for God, as well as such passages as Genesis 1:26; John 10:34 and 1 Corinthians 8:5,6.

The following dialogue is based on actual conversations between Mormons and Christians. It illustrates the Mormon attempt to prove Mormon doctrine and possible Christian/biblical responses.[13]

Mormon: We do believe that our God is one among many gods.

Christian: Where do you find that in the Bible?

Mormon: Well, the very fact that God's name in the Old Testament, *Elohim*, is plural in the Hebrew, indicates there are gods.

Christian: It is true that *Elohim* is plural in form in the Hebrew, but when it is used of the God of the Bible, it is regularly followed by a singular verb, indicating that *Elohim* is one. Furthermore, a singular pronoun is used with *Elohim*. For example, in Genesis 17:8 we read, "I will be their God *(Elohim)*," not We. Again, in Exodus 3:14, "God *(Elohim)* said to Moses, 'I Am Who I Am,'" Not "We are Who We are." You see, in the Bible, though *Elohim* is plural in form it is singular in construction and in meaning. Therefore, it speaks of only one true God, not many as you claim.

Mormon: You have chosen some verses that would seem to support your belief.

Christian: Excuse me, but in virtually every case in which the name of God—*Elohim*—is used, this is the case, not just the two verses which I mentioned.

Mormon: Well, that may be, but what about Genesis 1:26 which clearly teaches that there are many gods? "Then God *[Elohim]* said, 'Let *us* make man in *our* image, according to *our* likeness.'" There the pronoun is plural.

Christian: Please do not stop with verse 26. It is always easy to lift a verse out of context and make it say whatever one wishes. Read verse 27.

Mormon: O.K. "And God created man in His own image,

120

in the image of God He created him; male and female He created them."

Christian: Now, take note of what you read. "God created man in *His* own image." That is the second person singular form. If *Elohim* means gods, should it not read "their own image"? The "us" and "our" in Genesis 1:26 refers to the plurality within the one true God ("His" in verse 27), or as the Bible teaches, three Persons—Father, Son and Holy Spirit—in one true God. Therefore this passage supports the biblical doctrine of the triune God.

Mormon: But didn't Jesus say, "You are gods," in John 10:34?

Christian: Why don't you read the entire verse for us?

Mormon: O.K. "Jesus answered them, 'Has it not been written in your Law, "I said, you are gods"?' "

Christian: What passage from the Old Testament is Jesus referring to?

Mormon: Let's see—Psalm 82:6.

Christian: Jesus is speaking to the Pharisees and He quotes Psalm 82:6. What were these gods which Jesus mentioned?

Mormon: Gods are gods!

Christian: Really? In Psalm 82:2 these gods were those who "judge unjustly, and show partiality to the wicked." Does that sound like God?

Mormon: Well—

Christian: And in verse 7 God Himself says of these gods, "You will die like men." Can God die? How could these be gods? The only conceivable answer is that they were called gods because they held the office of God's representatives. They were not gods by nature, as only the one true eternal God of the Bible is.

Mormon: Let's get down to the clear teaching of the Bible. The apostle Paul tells us, and you should be able to see this, that "indeed there are many gods and many lords, yet for us there is but one God, the Father, from whom are all things" (1 Cor. 8:5,6). That is the Mormon doctrine of God. There are many gods, but there is only one God of this earth, only one God for *us.*

Christian: Perhaps if you read the latter part of verse 4 and the entire passage in verse 5 it would clarify what Paul is teaching.

Mormon: O.K. "There is no God but one. For even if there are so-called gods whether in heaven or on earth, as indeed there are many gods and many lords, yet for us there is but one God . . . "

Christian: That's fine. Note that Paul says, "There is no God but one." There is only one who by His own nature is God. Galatians 4:8 is also very clear on this point. Paul then goes on to say that there are many things which are called gods. You can call a tree "god" and man "god," but none of these gods is God by nature, for there is only one true God. Now, you have shared some passages which you claim teach your doctrine of many gods. Let me share with you what the Bible really teaches about God. Would you turn to Deuteronomy 6:4 please, and read it.

Mormon: "Hear, O Israel! The Lord is our God, the Lord is One!" This refers to the God of this earth.

Christian: If you turn to Isaiah 43:10 I think you will see there is only one true God.

Mormon: " 'You are My witnesses,' declares the Lord, 'and My servant whom I have chosen, in order that you may know and believe Me, and understand that I am He. Before Me there was no God formed, and there will be none after Me."

Christian: Think for a minute. Does God state here that there are any other gods in existence before Him?

Mormon: Well—

Christian: "Before Me there was no God formed." How about after? "And there will be none after Me." There is only one true God, and He Himself says that there are no other gods before Him nor any after Him. Look at Isaiah 44:6.

Mormon: "Thus says the Lord, the King of Israel and his Redeemer, the Lord of hosts: 'I am the first and I am the last, and there is no God besides Me.' "

Christian: Read verse 8.

Mormon: "Is there any God besides Me, or is there any other Rock? I know of none."

Christian: There are many other passages in Isaiah alone where God declares that He is the only God. You may believe that there are many gods, but there can be no doubt that the Bible teaches the existence of only one eternal true God.

What About the Trinity?

In addition to the above, Mormons will attack the doctrine of the Trinity, seeking to prove a tri-theism (three gods) rather than a triune God. A dialogue on this subject might go something like the following:

Christian: The Bible definitely teaches that within the nature of the one true God there are three eternal Persons: the Father, the Son, who is Jesus Christ, and the Holy Spirit.

Mormon: Now how can that be? Was Jesus a ventriloquist, projecting his voice up to heaven and saying, "This is My beloved Son, in whom I am wellpleased" (Matt. 3:17)? How can God stand at His own right hand? (See Acts 7:55.)

Christian: The essence of what God is, His very being, is in the Father and in the Son and in the Holy Spirit, all at the same time. God can be in more than one place at the same time (see Ps. 139:1-10; Jer. 23:24). Therefore, God can be in Jesus in the water being baptized, in the Father in heaven speaking, and in the Holy Spirit descending in the form of a dove simultaneously, with no problem whatever. He can be Jesus and the Father simul-

123

taneously while Jesus sits at the right hand of the Father. There is only one true God eternally existing in three Persons.

Mormon: Incredible!

Christian: Remember that we are trying to comprehend the infinite God of the Bible with our finite, limited minds. There can be no doubt that the Father, Jesus Christ and the Holy Spirit are one God.

Mormon: We agree that all three are God, but how can they be the same person? They can't be, and therefore they must be three gods.

Christian: They are not the same person. This is a common mistake Mormons make. They are three different Persons existing in one God.

Mormon: What about John 17:21 where Jesus prayed "that they may all be one; even as Thou, Father, art in Me, and I in Thee, that they also may be in Us"? Were all the disciples one blob? Of course not. They were one in purpose.

Christian: This prayer by Jesus is for the unity of believers, a supernatural oneness going beyond any oneness in purpose. The moment we believe, we are supernaturally baptized into the body of Jesus Christ—the church—and partake of the Holy Spirit, the third Person of the triune God who dwells in each believer. See 1 Corinthians 6:19; 12:13. It is more than just oneness in purpose; it is a supernatural link between believers through the Holy Spirit.

Mormon: Well—

Christian: Let's get back to the subject at hand. It is a firmly established fact in both the Old and New Testaments that there is only one true God. God is three Persons in one essence, each Person being fully God, yet distinct from each other. Jesus told us to baptize "in the name of the Father and the Son and the Holy Spirit" (Matt. 28:19). There is just one "name" (singular) and that name is triune: "the Father and the Son and the Holy Spirit."

Is God a Glorified Man?

Mormons will also attempt to demonstrate from the Bible that the God of this world, the Heavenly Father, is a glorified resurrected man having a body of flesh and bones. They use the anthropomorphisms of the Bible (passages where God is described with human characteristics), along with such passages as Exodus 24:9,10 and 33:11 where people have seen God "face to face." The following dialogue will illustrate some of the ways Mormons attempt to support their doctrine, and also responses which Christians could give.

Mormon: Have you ever read 1 Peter 3:12?

Christian: Let's see, "For the eyes of the Lord are upon the righteous, and His ears attend to their prayer, but the face of the Lord is against those who do evil."

Mormon: Did you ever notice how often the Bible ascribes human parts to God, such as eyes, ears, face, hands and feet?

Christian: Yes.

Mormon: Didn't you understand that God has a body of flesh and bones in those passages?

Christian: No. These are just metaphors describing God in the form of man. They are commonly known as anthropomorphisms. This is figurative language used to explain activities of God which are beyond our experience. They are not to be taken literally.

Mormon: We take the Bible very literally. It says what it says and we believe it!

Christian: Have you ever read Psalm 91:4 where it says of God "He will cover you with His pinions, and under His wings you may seek refuge"? Is God a large bird?

Mormon: Don't be absurd!

Christian: Shouldn't we take this literally?

Mormon: It is used to describe the activity of God.

Christian: Precisely, and that is exactly what anthropomorphisms are used for. God is no more a glorified man with a body of flesh and bones than He is a large bird.

Mormon: Did Jesus have a body?

Christian: Yes.

Mormon: Is Jesus God?

Christian: Yes.

Mormon: Then God has a body!

Christian: Jesus was God before He came to earth. He added to Himself a human nature, a body. The first chapter of John's Gospel, verses 1 and 14 make that quite clear.

Mormon: Do you believe that anyone has ever seen God?

Christian: John 1:18 says, "No man has seen God at any time." First John 4:12 states the same thing.

Mormon: Now this is getting ridiculous. Doesn't the Bible say that Moses, Aaron, Nadab, Abihu and the 70 elders of Israel saw the God of Israel standing on a pavement of sapphire? (See Exod. 24:9,10.)

Christian: Yes, but they did not see God Himself. They saw a theophany, or God-form. You see, God often assumed a human form for a particular purpose. He showed Himself in a form that made Himself (the invisible being of God) visible to the human eye. These are common in the Old Testament.

Mormon: A theophany?

Christian: Yes! For example, there is a theophany in the New Testament in which God the Holy Spirit came down at the baptism of Jesus "in bodily form like a dove" (Luke 3:22). This does not mean that the Holy Spirit always goes around in a dove's form any more than it means that a dove form exists within every believer. It means that the Holy Spirit assumed that form for that occasion.

Mormon: I suppose the next thing you will tell me is that

126

Moses saw a theophany in Exodus 33:11. There it states, and you can read it for yourself. "Thus the Lord used to speak to Moses face to face, just as a man speaks to his friend."

Christian: This is another instance of a theophany.

Mormon: If you are planning to use verse 20 to support your idea—where God says, "You cannot see My face, for no man can see Me and live!"—then you have a contradiction in the Bible to deal with. How could Moses speak to God "face to face" and not see His face?

Christian: The phrase "face to face" is an expression of intimacy, and it appropriately explains the closeness of the relationship between Moses and God. Therefore, it is not contradictory to verse 20, for Moses did not see the face of God. Many passages in the Bible make it clear that God is not a glorified man. God Himself expressly denies being a man. Look at Hosea 11:9.

Mormon: "I am God and not man, the Holy One in your midst."

Christian: God is not a glorified man; rather He is Spirit. Read John 4:24.

Mormon: "God is spirit."

Christian: Now let's define what spirit is. Look at Luke 24:39.

Mormon: "For a spirit does not have flesh and bones as you see that I have."

Christian: Right. If God is spirit, and a spirit does not have flesh and bones, then God does not have a body of flesh and bones. Consider the greatness of the invisible one true God. Read Jeremiah 23:24.

Mormon: " 'Do I not fill the heaven and the earth?' declares the Lord."

Christian: Now, if God had a body of flesh and bones this would be an interesting sight, wouldn't it?

Mormon: I guess so.

Christian: Second Chronicles 6:18 says the same thing.

"Behold, heaven and the highest heaven cannot contain thee." God is not a glorified man. He is Spirit. Furthermore, He never was a man. Psalm 90:2 says, "Before the mountains were born, or Thou didst give birth to the earth and the world, even from everlasting to everlasting, Thou art God." As God will always be God, so He always was God.

The glorified human gods of Mormonism cannot in any way be compared to the God of the Bible. Because they are glorified men with bodies of flesh and blood, they cannot be present everywhere. Because they are still progressing in what is called eternal progression, they are not all-powerful. They do not even know everything. Such a limited view of God is the consequence of exchanging "the glory of the incorruptible God for an image in the form of corruptible man" (Rom. 1:23).

How majestic by comparison is the one true God of the Bible. As the psalmist writes, "Where can I go from Thy Spirit? Or where can I flee from Thy presence? If I ascend to heaven Thou art there; . . . Thine eyes have seen my unformed substance; and in Thy book they were all written, the days that were ordained for me, when as yet there was not one of them. How precious also are Thy thoughts to me, O God! How vast is the sum of them! If I should count them, they would outnumber the sand" (Ps. 139:7,8,16-18).

When talking with Mormons, keep in mind that Mormons will attempt to support their beliefs about God by reinterpreting Bible passages in the light of their preconceived theology. They will also redefine biblical terms. They will claim to believe in an eternal God when they believe that God was once a man, and that there was a time when God was not God. They will claim to believe in one God when they mean one God for us on earth among many gods. They will claim to believe in the Trinity, when they mean tri-theism or three gods.

Therefore, it is important for you to know what Mormons believe about God so you will be able to clarify what they say and then present to them the truth about God from His Word, the Bible. There is but one true eternal God whose essence is spirit and who exists in three Persons: the Father, the Son and the Holy Spirit.

Reflection
1. Does it make any difference what doctrine of God one believes? Why?'
2. Summarize the Mormon doctrine of God. In what areas is it different from the Bible?
3. Do you think you are capable right now of responding effectively to the Mormon doctrine of God? Where could you strengthen yourself so that you would be able to share your faith more effectively to them?

Projects and Proofs
1. Make a list of passages from the Bible which you could use and explain to show the Mormons what the Bible teaches about God.
2. Create a magazine ad or television commercial on the greatness of the biblical God in contrast to the God of Mormonism.

Thinking Ahead
While visiting your library, you notice a Mormon book on the shelf by James E. Talmage entitled *Articles of Faith* (36th Edition, Salt Lake City, Utah: The Church of Jesus Christ of Latter-day Saints, 1957). You open it up to pages 478, 479 where you read, "Redemption from personal sins can only be obtained through obedience to the requirements of the gospel, and a life of good works." How is this different from what the Bible teaches?

What passages would you use to show what the Bible teaches?

129

Notes

1. See *Doctrines and Covenants*, 93:33, "The Elements Are Eternal" and the Mormon chart, "The Mormon Plan of Eternal Progression"; cf. also Sterling M. McMurrin, *The Philosophical Foundations of Mormon Theology* (University of Utah Press, 1959), p. 12, 29.

2. Hunter, *op. cit.*, pp. 126-129.

3. Bruce McConkie, *Mormon Doctrine*, p. 156.

4. Pratt, *op. cit.*, pp. 23,132.

5. See Joseph Smith, Jr., *Times and Seasons* (August 1, 1844); *Journal of Discourses*, vol. 1, p. 123; 4, pp. 3,4; and Joseph Fielding Smith, compiler, *Teachings of the Prophet Joseph Smith*, p. 345.

6. Ora Pate Steward, *We Believe*, p. 11.

7. Hunter, *op. cit.*, p. 98; cf. Talmage, *op. cit.*, p. 443.

8. Talmage, *op. cit.*, p. 430.

9. Young, *Journal of Discourses*, vol. 3, p. 93.

10. Pratt, *Journal of Discourses*, vol. 2, p. 345.

11. Joseph Fielding Smith, *op. cit.*, p. 370.

12. Joseph Smith, Jr., April 6, 1843 in N.B. Lundwell, comp., *Discourses on the Holy Spirit*, p. 73.

13. The material used in these dialogues is from taped interviews between Mormons and students of Northeastern Bible College. Some material also used from Wally Tope, "Maximizing Your Witness to Mormons," *Contemporary Christianity*, vol. 7, no. 3 (September-November, 1977), pp. 2-11.

13

ONE MAY BE SAVED, BUT...

One night a very respected Jewish leader named Nicodemus visited Jesus. Nicodemus was a Pharisee and a ruler of the Jews. Jesus looked right through him, seeing him as a sinner in need of a restored relationship with God, and said to him, "Truly, truly . . . unless one is born again, he cannot see the kingdom of God" (John 3:3). Jesus' statement, that he needed to be "born again," confused Nicodemus and he wondered how he could "enter a second time into his mother's womb and be born" (John 3:4). But Jesus was not speaking of another physical birth. He was speaking of a spiritual birth. As a sinner, Nicodemus needed to be saved and brought into a relationship with God. And what was Nicodemus to do to be saved or be born again? Jesus said, "God so loved the world, that He gave His only begotten Son, that whoever believes in Him should not perish, but have eternal life" (John 3:16).

Jesus Christ knew that Nicodemus was a sinner, as all people are, and that sin separated him from God. In order to be restored to a relationship with God, Nicodemus must

131

experience a spiritual birth. Jesus said one must be born again by the Spirit of God, which is accomplished by believing in Him. This, then, is the biblical teaching of salvation: sinful man is brought into relationship with God by faith in Jesus Christ.

If Nicodemus had met some Mormons on that night, how would they have seen him in his relationship to God? What would they have told him he must do to be saved? What is the Mormon doctrine of salvation?

Original Sin

In the Mormon scheme of salvation man is not sinful as a result of what Adam did in the Garden in Eden, for Mormons do not believe that Adam sinned in originally breaking God's law. They believe it is possible to break a law of God without committing sin, as was Adam's case.[1] However there were effects as a result of Adam's original action that have touched all of mankind, effects such as death. This is the Mormon doctrine of the fall of man.

By eliminating the original sin of Adam and thereby the fact that all of mankind became sinful as a result of Adam's disobedience, Mormons focus their attention on the personal sins they commit for which they will be punished. This, of course, shifts their focus from the idea that they are essentially sinners by nature to the idea that they are gods in embryo—the doctrine of eternal progression.

This brings us to the Mormon doctrine of salvation, of which there are two kinds.[2] The first is a general or unconditional salvation which is synonymous with resurrection. The second is an individual or personal salvation which, in its fullest form, is synonymous with exaltation or man progressing to godhood.

General Salvation = Resurrection

Since one result of the fall is that everyone dies, general salvation is necessary to redeem everyone from death. Obviously, redeeming mankind from death requires resurrection. This salvation or resurrection is automatic and is granted to every person without any necessary act on his or her part. Belief in Jesus Christ is not an issue.[3] Even the wicked will be saved in that they will be resurrected.[4] All mankind (with the exception of the "sons of perdition")[5] will be resurrected and judged at the resurrection by their works. Depending on what they have done, they will receive a part in either the telestial or terrestrial kingdom. Those who have a part only in this general salvation or resurrection are considered by the Mormon church to be "damned."[6]

Individual Salvation = Exaltation

Since people do commit personal sins, a personal or individual salvation is needed to redeem people from these sins. What does Mormonism propose as a solution to personal sins? Mormonism says, "Redemption from personal sins can only be obtained through obedience to the requirement of the gospel, and a life of good works."[7]

Individual salvation, therefore, is one which man merits by obedience to the laws and ordinances of the gospel. But more than that, it is what man must do in order to attain godhood. Individual salvation, in its fullest form, is exaltation, i.e., progressing to godhood.

What must a person do in order to merit forgiveness from personal sins and attain godhood?

Following is a list of Mormon requirements:

1. Faith in Jesus Christ.
2. Repentance.
3. Baptism—this is the beginning of the process of moving toward godhood when one is born again in Mormonism.[8]
4. Laying on of hands—the ceremony for conferring priesthoods (indicating a transfer of authority and powers to that person).

133

5. Church membership—one cannot be saved, in the sense of exaltation or attaining godhood, outside the Church of Jesus Christ of Latter-day Saints.[9]
6. Keeping the commandments—this includes such areas as the Ten Commandments, the Word of Wisdom (refraining from the use of tea, coffee, tobacco, alcohol, etc.), tithing, gaining knowledge, being fruitful and multiplying, being virtuous and morally clean, doing good works in general, and obeying all the commands and directions given by the leaders of the church.
7. Accepting Joseph Smith and His Successors as "God's mouthpiece"—there can be no salvation in the sense of exaltation without accepting Joseph Smith, Jr.[10]
8. Temple work—this includes being married in the Mormon Temple, having your whole family sealed together (spiritually united as a family for all eternity), doing genealogical work in tracing your family back as far as possible, and performing saving ordinances in the Temple for those who have died—such as proxy baptism, sealing, ordination and endowments (specifically temple work which is done by Mormons for themselves or for direct descendants who have died).

According to Mormonism your status after death will all depend upon your good conduct. Whether you become a god or not, or which of the three glories you will dwell in is determined by your life, works and obedience here on earth.

Three Degrees of Glory

Mormons believe that there are three kingdoms mankind will occupy one day.[11] The lowest is the Telestial Kingdom, where an endless host of people will dwell. These will include those who were liars, thieves, adulterers and murderers.[12]

The next is the Terrestrial Kingdom, where those who were "honorable" people but who did not accept the Mormon gospel in this life will dwell. Some Mormon writings indicate that these "honorable" people must change their minds in the spirit world and accept the Mormon gospel to be included in this kingdom.[13]

The highest is the Celestial Kingdom, which is eternal life. This Kingdom is only for Mormons. There are three heavens or degrees in this kingdom, and only those who have been married in the Mormon Temple may have part in the highest.[14] They will enter the highest heaven in family units and become gods.[15]

In summary, the Mormon doctrine of salvation teaches that everyone will be resurrected and redeemed from the devil. Furthermore, salvation is a process in which each individual can, through his or her own efforts, earn forgiveness from God for wrongs done. This is accomplished by keeping the commandments. Having faith is a commandment to be kept. Repenting, being baptized, receiving the laying on of hands, and so on, are all commandments to be kept. A man can actually attain godhood if he has fulfilled all of these requirements.

Is Salvation for Everyone?

Knowing that so many of the areas included in their doctrine of salvation do not appear in the Bible, Mormons generally lift certain passages out of context or reinterpret them in the light of their preconceived theology in an attempt to biblically prove certain aspects of their doctrine of salvation.

Mormons will try to prove their doctrine of general salvation or resurrection by referring to such passages as Romans 5:18; 1 Corinthians 15:22 and 1 Timothy 4:10, which seem to teach a universal salvation.

Romans 5:18 says, "So then as through one transgression there resulted condemnation to all men; even so through one act of righteousness there resulted justification of life to all men." While Mormons will interpret this as meaning that all are saved, the Bible clearly teaches that this is not the case. The context of Romans 5 is speaking of those who have been justified by faith (v. 1) and thus the parallelism in Romans 5:18 should be understood in this way: all who are condemned (and this includes the whole human race) are condemned because of the sin of Adam; all who are justified (and justification is by faith) are justified because of the righteousness of Jesus Christ.

First Corinthians 15:22 says, "For as in Adam all die, so in Christ all shall be made alive." Mormons claim that this teaches that all will be resurrected and therefore saved. But the next verse tells us that the "all" who "shall be made alive" are those who are Christ's at His coming. Thus the passage is not referring to the resurrection of all mankind but only of those who belong to Jesus Christ.

First Timothy 4:10 says, "We have fixed our hope on the living God, who is the Savior of all men, especially of believers." While Mormons focus on the phrase "the Savior of all men," proclaiming a salvation for all men, they seem to miss the qualifying phrase "especially of believers." The Bible draws distinction which could be stated in this manner: God is the Saviour of all in a potential sense, and Saviour of those who believe in an actual sense. What Jesus accomplished on Calvary's cross is available to all, but appropriated only to those who by faith alone have personally accepted Him as Saviour.

What About the Individual?

Mormons will also try to prove their doctrine of individual salvation by referring to such passages as James 2:17 and Revelation 20:13, which seem to state the necessity of works for salvation.

James 2:17 says, "Even so faith, if it has no works, is dead, being by itself." Mormons use this passage to show that faith alone is insufficient and therefore works (good deeds) are necessary for salvation. In this passage James is distinguishing between two types of faith: a false faith in which one knows about God but doesn't act upon the knowledge—a dead faith; and the true faith in which one believes and acts upon that belief by accepting Jesus Christ as Saviour and Lord— saving faith. Saving faith will eventually result in a life that produces good works. In this light, works is the visible working out of faith and the proof of a real and genuine faith in Jesus Christ. But salvation is in no way earned by works; salvation is still by faith in Jesus Christ.

Revelation 20:13 says, "And the sea gave up the dead which were in it, and death and Hades gave up the dead which were in them; and they were judged, every one of them according to their deeds." While Mormons will claim that this passage teaches that all will be judged according to their works, the context of Revelation 20 will not allow for this.

In Revelation 20:13 the unbelievers are the ones who will be judged by what they have done and their works will be the evidence that will prove them deserving of the lake of fire (see Rev. 21:8).

Mormons might well reply, "But Christians are judged by their works, aren't they?" It is true that Christians will be judged for their works, but this is with regard to rewards they will receive in heaven, and not with regard to salvation (1 Cor. 3:11-15 makes this quite clear). Salvation is not based on works but faith in Jesus Christ. Salvation is not earned; it is a gift to those who have true faith in Jesus Christ (see Eph. 2:8,9).

What About Baptism?

In addition to using these references, Mormons will try to demonstrate the necessity of water baptism for salvation by referring to such passages as Acts 2:38 and 22:16.

Acts 2:38 says, "Repent, and let each of you be baptized in the name of Jesus Christ for the forgiveness of your sins." Mormons use this passage to teach that baptism is necessary for forgiveness of sins. The meaning of this passage is clearer if we understand that the preposition "for" could be translated "on the basis of." This use of the preposition would be similar to the following: "When you take an aspirin *for* a headache, it's *not* to *get* a headache; but it's because you've *already got* one."[16] Or, to put it in terms of Acts 2:38: Be baptized in the name of Jesus on the basis that you have already received forgiveness of sin (by faith in Jesus Christ). This understanding of Acts 2:38 is supported by many passages in the rest of the Bible, which teach that faith in Jesus Christ, not baptism, is the basis for forgiveness of sins.

Acts 22:16 says, "Arise, and be baptized, and wash away your sins, calling on His name." While Mormons link the washing away of sins with being baptized, the natural connection is with "calling on His name," which would bring about forgiveness of sins.

What About the Three Kingdoms?

Finally, Mormons will try to prove their doctrine of the Three Kingdoms or Glories—the Telestial, Terrestrial, and Celestial—by referring to 1 Corinthians 15:40,41: "There are also heavenly bodies and earthly bodies, but the glory of the heavenly is one, and the glory of the earthly is another. There is one glory of the sun, and another glory of the moon, and another glory of the stars; for star differs from star in glory." Stressing the fact that there are three glories mentioned in verse 41, Mormons claim this is a reference to their three kingdoms. However, the entire context of 1 Corinthians 15 is speaking of resurrection, and verses 35-54 specifically refer to resurrection bodies. Verse 40, then, speaks of the difference between the body we now possess and the body we will have; and verse 41 speaks of the varieties of resurrected bodies, as verses 42-44 clearly indicate.

138

What Does the Bible Say?

Being able to respond to the Scriptures which Mormons refer to is effective and helpful, but you must also be able to show them what the Bible really teaches about salvation.

Remember that sin entered the world through one man, Adam, and through this sin the judgment of God came upon all mankind. The tragedy of the fall went far beyond Adam and Eve, affecting mankind as a whole. Romans 5:12 says, "Through one man sin entered into the world, and death through sin." People are essentially sinful beings not only because of Adam, but because of sins people continually commit against God.

Point out to the Mormon that Jesus came into the world to save sinners (see 1 Tim. 1:15), not to provide resurrection for all. To say merely that all men are saved because all are resurrected is directly contradictory to God's Word, the Bible. In John 5:28,29, we read, "All who are in the tombs shall hear His voice, and shall come forth; those who did the good deeds to a resurrection of life, those who committed the evil deeds to a resurrection of judgment." Is the resurrection of judgment a resurrection to glory? Likewise, is the broad road which leads to destruction in Matthew 7:13,14 a kingdom of glory?

Jesus said, "He who believes in the Son has eternal life; but he who does not obey the Son shall not see life, but the wrath of God abides on him" (John 3:36). Those who refuse to accept His words and believe in Him as Lord and Saviour will one day hear Jesus say, "Depart from Me, accursed ones, into the eternal fire which has been prepared for the devil and his angels" (Matt. 25:41).

Keep in mind that no one can be saved by achievements or accomplishments. Despite their scrupulous attempts to keep the Law, no Jews have ever made it to heaven by keeping the commandments (see Rom. 3:20), and neither will anyone else. Galatians 2:16 makes this clear: "A man is not justified by the works of the Law but through faith

139

in Christ Jesus, . . . by the works of the Law shall no flesh be justified."

Neither can works save or justify anyone before God. Ephesians 2:8,9 makes this clear, "For by grace you have been saved through faith; and that not of yourselves, it is the gift of God; not as a result of works, that no one should boast."

The apostle Paul speaks of such futile attempts to attain righteousness in Romans 10:3, where he says, "For not knowing about God's righteousness, and seeking to establish their own, they did not subject themselves to the righteousness of God."

There is a pride in us which wants to say, "I earned it," or, "Look at what I have accomplished." But God will not allow this, for it is God who has provided for our complete salvation in Jesus Christ. This salvation is a gift from God, appropriated to all who by faith have accepted Jesus Christ as Lord and Saviour.

Contrary to the Mormon doctrine of salvation, the thief on the cross entered into Paradise[17] unbaptized, without any good works, temple works or religion. He simply trusted in Christ alone for salvation (see Luke 23:42,43). It is in this light that we must proclaim again the good news of the gospel. Jesus said, "Unless one is born again, he cannot see the kingdom of God" (John 3:3).

As to how one is truly saved and born again, the apostle Paul simply states, "Believe in the Lord Jesus, and you shall be saved" (Acts 16:31).

Reflection

1. Does it make any difference what way one thinks he can be saved? Why?
2. Summarize the Mormon doctrine of salvation. How is the biblical doctrine different? How would you approach the task of showing a Mormon from the Bible what true salvation is? What passages would you use?

Projects and Proofs

1. Outline the various aspects of the Mormon doctrine of salvation on one half of a sheet of paper. On the other half write down thoughts and passages from the Bible which would be helpful in showing a Mormon that his/her scheme of salvation differs from what the Bible teaches.

2. Create a presentation of the biblical plan of salvation leading a person to accepting Jesus Christ as Lord and Saviour. Use the materials in this book and other sources. Be sure to have responses to those who say they can be saved by works or the keeping of the commandments. Practice presenting this with someone, perhaps a classmate, friend or member of your family.

Notes

1. McConkie, *Mormon Doctrine*, p. 804.
2. *Ibid.*, pp. 669, 670.
3. McConkie, *What Mormons Think of Christ*, pp. 24, 25.
4. McConkie, *Mormon Doctrine*, p. 671.
5. Although this group is not defined in Mormon writings, Mormons will generally define them verbally as those who have betrayed Mormonism or revealed Temple secrets.
6. McConkie, *Mormon Doctrine*, p. 669.
7. Talmage, *The Articles of Faith*, pp. 478, 479.
8. McConkie, *Mormon Doctrine*, p. 84.
9. *Ibid.*, p. 670.
10. Joseph Fielding Smith, *Doctrines of Salvation*, vol. 1, pp. 188-190.
11. *Doctrine and Covenants*, 76.
12. McConkie, *Mormon Doctrine*, pp. 778, 779.
13. *Ibid.*, p. 784.
14. *Ibid.*, p. 116, 117.
15. *Ibid.*, p. 670.
16. Wally Tope, *op. cit.*
17. See Luke 23:43. Paradise is referred to as the "third heaven" in 2 Corinthians 12:2,4. The three heavens in the Bible seem to be the atmosphere, the stars and planets and the place where God works from within His creation. The third heaven refers to the latter.

SECTION IV

NOW YOU CAN OPEN THE DOOR

A Christian response to the counterfeits

14

COUNTERFEITS AT YOUR DOOR!

Every counterfeit fails its holder at a crucial time, the time he tries to "spend" it. Likewise, while many religions make promises about eternal life, the eventual consequence of counterfeit faith is eternal separation from God. A Christian who meets a counterfeit at the door—or on the job or on campus—has a God-given opportunity to prevent someone who is precious in the eyes of God from suffering that consequence.

Every Christian is to share his or her faith in Jesus Christ, to tell others of the wonderful salvation He has provided, which they can have through faith in Him. Christians are here to present Jesus Christ and His salvation, inviting people to place their trust in Him as their Saviour and Lord. It is while Christians are doing this that the difference between real and counterfeit biblical faith becomes clear. Moreover, the eternal destiny of individuals belonging to counterfeit religious movements depends on their understanding that difference. They need the opportunity to know Jesus Christ and accept salvation through Him.

In today's religious diversity and confusion, the counterfeits are well disguised and more difficult to detect than in the past. In order to detect counterfeits and perhaps help someone to learn about salvation, watch for some of these problems in talking with him or her.

Be Aware of the Language Game

Many members of unorthodox religious groups use familiar Christian words and phrases but mean entirely different things by those terms. Moreover, it is easy to hear familiar Christian words and assume that the speaker defines those words the same way you do. For example, we have already seen that Jehovah's Witnesses and Mormons use the same words Christians use—God, Jesus, salvation, etc. However, both groups have very different understandings of these words from those presented in the Bible.

Another of the many members of unorthodox religious groups that use familiar terms differently is The Way International. These very friendly individuals give the impression that they are serious students of the Word of God, that they love Jesus and you, and that they are Christian. Their conversation will be punctuated with the "right" phrases, such as "the Lord Jesus Christ," "the blood of Jesus," "the Son of God," "the Holy Spirit," "the authority of the Word of God," and even an occasional "Praise the Lord!"—*but all with different meanings.*

Don't be fooled by them! While using the phrase "the Lord Jesus Christ," The Way International rejects His being God.[1] To them calling Jesus "the Son of God" indicates that He was a specially-created human being, created in the womb of the virgin Mary by God.[2] Jesus is "eternal" not because He preexisted with God, but because He always existed in the knowledge or mind of God.[3]

145

The Way International teaches that "the Holy Spirit" is another name for God the Father, just as Bob can be another name for Robert. For them, the Holy Spirit (capitalized) is not the same as the holy spirit (not capitalized), which is a gift God gives.[4] For them, the Holy Spirit is not the third Person of the triune Godhead, nor is Jesus the second Person of the Godhead.

Do you see how The Way International uses common Christian terms while meaning something completely different? Even Victor Paul Wierwille, founder and teacher of The Way International, tells us this. He says, "We must define our terms. Many people may be misled because, while using the same language or words, we don't mean the same thing."[5]

To avoid being fooled and to detect the counterfeit usage of words:

1. Remember that a word can be understood differently by different people.
2. Ask questions. "What do you mean by _____?" "Who is Jesus Christ, as you see Him?" "Can you tell me how one is born again as you understand it?"
3. Then to determine whether a statement is Christian or not, compare it with what the Bible says—all of the Bible, not just one or two passages.
4. Don't assume people are Christians because they use Christian terms.
5. Present the truth. Eternal destiny is at stake.

Avoid the Reinterpretation Game

In communicating the gospel try to understand what is going on in the mind of the individual you are talking with. Remember that communication is not so much what you say, but what that person understands you to say—and there is a difference! You have probably had many experiences, some very funny, in which you used all the right words and still had a person totally misunderstand what

146

you said because he or she gave your words a different meaning or context. Do you remember when you said _____ _____, and someone thought you said _____? It happens all the time.

It is easy for people to give their own meaning and interpretation to what they hear. And the same problem can occur when you are talking about your faith. People with different preconceived theologies may listen to the words you say, redefine the meaning in their minds so the words fit their own ideas. Such misunderstandings occurred even in the early church. In Acts 14:7-10 Paul and Barnabas are in Lystra preaching the gospel with all clarity and boldness. God even demonstrated His mighty power in the healing of a man who had been lame all of his life. But verses 11-13 reveal that the people did not fully understand either the gospel Paul and Barnabas preached or the healing. Those who heard the gospel and saw God's power demonstrated, reinterpreted the information in the light of their own religion and therefore tried to make Paul and Barnabas gods, calling them Zeus and Hermes (see Acts 14:12). Although the words were clear, the people did not understand what was said because they were caught in the reinterpretation game.

Consider the examples of this game we have already seen as we considered Jehovah's Witnesses and Mormons—both in their Bible study (selecting and reinterpreting passages based on their preconceived ideas) and in the dialogues. Words and phrases filtered through their preconceived theology acquired different meanings from those presented in the Bible.

Also consider the reinterpretations in the following discussion between a member of Sun Myung Moon's Unification Church and a Christian. The content in the parentheses defines what both the Christian and the Moonie mean, explaining the reinterpretation and deception which are occurring:[6]

Moonie: Would you like to make a donation to a worthy missionary cause?

Christian: I'm very much interested in missions, but first let me tell you about my wonderful Lord and Saviour Jesus Christ.

Moonie: Oh tremendous. I believe in Jesus Christ.

Christian: Do you believe that He is deity (God)?

Moonie: Absolutely! (divine, but not God[7]).

Christian: Did Jesus Christ die for your sins on Calvary's cross (redemption completed)?

Moonie: Oh yes! (redemption incomplete[8]) It is essential to us too that He rose up from the dead (as a spirit man, not physically[9]).

Christian: It is essential for me too (physical resurrection)! Do you believe He (Jesus) is coming again to this earth?

Moonie: We believe Christ (Moon[10]) is coming again (physically born on this earth). We love the Lord (Moon) and pray in His name (Moon[11]) all the time.

Christian: Isn't He (Jesus) a tremendous Saviour and Lord? Tell me, when were you "born again" (saved by faith in Jesus alone)?

Moonie: I've been born again (learning doctrine) for over two years now. Say, why don't you come up to one of our workshops and get on fire for Christ (Moon) and learn more about Him (Moon)?

Tremendous conversation, isn't it? That member of the Unification Church never heard the gospel as the Bible presents it, but only a reinterpretation of it which makes it the same as Unification theology. Remember, if he sees no differences between what a Christian is saying and what he believes (because of reinterpretation), no evangelism can take place.

How can we prevent this reinterpretation from taking place?

Speak about specific differences between what the Bible says and what the groups teach. In Acts 14:14-17, when

148

Paul and Barnabas realized that reinterpretation had taken place, they began to proclaim the difference between Christian theology and that which the people believed. "We are also men of the same nature as you, and preach the gospel to you in order that you should turn from these vain things to a living God, who made the heaven and the earth and the sea, and all that is in them" (Acts 14:15). Be able to say, "Here is what the unorthodox religious group teaches and this is what the Bible teaches." Acts 14:18 reveals the difficulty in getting people to see there is a difference, but unless the differences are out in the open so a person can consider the uniqueness of biblical Christianity, there can be no evangelism.

Ask questions to determine what others hear you saying. Do not let people reinterpret what you are saying without checking for counterfeit interpretations. Do not be afraid to probe. Raise questions. Ask for their understanding of what you said.

Don't Be Fooled by the Esoteric Game

There is a third trap to consider in sharing your faith with members of unorthodox religious groups. Many religious movements today present a public theology which is different from the esoteric or private theology of the group. What you hear in public may not be what the group actually believes and teaches. It is easy to hear familiar Christian doctrine and assume that these people are Christian, when their real and private teachings are actually contrary to what is presented in the Bible.

A classic example of this is the Local Church, whose founder and leader is Witness Lee. Consider their doctrine of God and the Trinity. To the Christian public the Local Church declares: "We believe that God is the only one Triune God—the Father, the Son, and the Holy Spirit—co-existing equally from eternity to eternity."[12] Sounds great.

Yet privately they teach that "the three Persons of the

149

Trinity became the three successive stages in the process of God's economy. Without these three stages, God's essence could never be dispensed into man."[13] In other words, God manifested Himself as the Father, then as the Son and then as the Holy Spirit. (This theology contradicts their public claim that the Father, Son and Holy Spirit coexist eternally.) Furthermore, the Local Church teaches that the purpose of Jesus' becoming flesh was for God to become man and through this "mingling" of God with man, as they refer to it, for man to become God. Lee writes, "God's desire is not that man should be only a good man, but much more, a GOD-man, one who is the same as He is . . . . Because we have the life of God in us we can be what God is and do what God does . . . . "[14] It is only logical that if we become God, we must also become a part of the Godhead. So Lee also writes: "There are now four in one: the Father, the Son, the Spirit, and the Body."[15] (This contradicts their public claim to believe in only one triune God.)

This difference between public and private teachings presents problems for someone trying to detect religious counterfeits such as the Local Church. Accepting the Christian side of their theology leads to being fooled by a counterfeit. Detecting the counterfeit—the other side of their theology—means they will tell you that you are taking the quotes out of context and misrepresenting them. To make things worse, they will even quote the seemingly Christian or public side of their theology as proof against the private or counterfeit side. To avoid being fooled:

Have some knowledge of the teaching of these groups if possible. In dealing with the Local Church, it is possible to help one of their members who might truly be a Christian to see the discrepancy between their public and private teachings and thus help that person learn about God's truth.

When in doubt about the teaching of a group, be as thorough as possible in asking questions about their beliefs.

150

Expect the Deception Game

Anticipate groups that teach their members to be deceptive. For example, members of the Unification Church have been known to practice "heavenly deception," as they call it. This has been based on the teaching that since Satan deceived God's children, they, as God's children, are justified in deceiving Satan's children (those not of their unorthodox religious group).

Be Prepared for Pseudo-Scholarship Games

Another common game is pseudo-scholarship which overwhelms the listener with all kind of seemingly sound facts and statistics. For example, The Way International is well-equipped to quote the Greek and Aramaic languages, often inaccurately, and use church history to back up their preconceived theology.

Many groups reinterpret biblical passages. Expect to be confronted often with the challenge, "That's your interpretation," or "That's the way you look at the Bible." For example, a Christian may use John 14:6 to demonstrate the uniqueness of Jesus Christ to a person in an eastern religion who believes divinity is in all human beings. But a teacher in Transcendental Meditation will probably respond by lifting the words of Jesus out of context and changing the meaning. "Yes, Jesus said 'I am the way, and the truth, and the life; no one comes to the Father, but through Me.' And we should all say the same of ourselves in recognition of finding the divineness within ourselves by meditating." The passage actually refers to the uniqueness of Jesus, but the reinterpreter has twisted it to teach that we are all divine.

It is important to have standards for interpreting Scripture. For example, without resorting to sarcasm or a judgmental tone, learn to recognize and explain the difference between interpretations that are consistent and those that are inconsistent with the rest of the Bible.

151

Check interpretations by looking them up in works of a variety of reliable scholars.

Never accept a seemingly foreign interpretation on the spot. Ask for time to think about it and do some research.

In Summary

It is true that members of unorthodox religious groups often use the same terms Christians use. They might reinterpret statements of doctrine and biblical passages. They might seek to overwhelm with false scholarship. They might even willingly deceive or not reveal their whole theology. But continue to present the person and work of Jesus Christ and invite people to accept Him as their personal Lord and Saviour.

Be able to explain why you are a Christian, what it means to you to have Jesus as your Lord and Saviour. Share about your personal relationship with God through Jesus and about the joy, peace, security, forgiveness, meaning, etc., that the relationship gives you. A personal joy about your own living relationship with a living Lord is one of the strongest tools you have.

Remember the power of prayer and use it. You are presenting God's truth to people, but the Holy Spirit convicts the heart and brings about conversion (see 1 Cor. 3:6,7; John 16:8-10). Seek His help. Pray before talking with members of unorthodox religious groups. Pray while talking with these people. If you are with a friend, pray while your friend talks. Pray after talking with members of unorthodox religious groups.

Meet people where they are spiritually. Though members of religious movements have different needs and are at different stages of doubting or accepting beliefs and practices, they all had a point of entry—that is, a reason they entered that particular movement.

Be aware of why or how each person has chosen his or her religious movement and the implications. Then speak to that issue. For example, in becoming a Jehovah's Witness a person accepts the absolute authority (accuracy) of the Watchtower publications they study (not the Bible). Therefore, help these people see the false teachings in those publications. Help them see that the Bible is a more reliable source of authority. In becoming Mormons, many people base their decision on subjective feelings—I prayed about it; Mormons are such good people; they are such a fine organization. Help these people see that feelings and being "good people" are not tests for truth. Only God's Word is.

Remember your goal. A Christian is helping people hear about and understand the uniqueness and greatness of Jesus Christ and His salvation. The goal is to help people know Jesus personally and accept His salvation.

Be a representative of Jesus Christ to a lost and dying world. Do not be "quarrelsome" (literally "to do verbal battle"), but "be kind to all, able to teach, patient when wronged, with gentleness correcting those who are in opposition; if perhaps God may grant them repentance leading to the knowledge of the truth, and they may come to their senses and escape from the snare of the devil, having been held captive by him to do his will" (2 Tim. 2:24-26).

Notes

1. Victor Paul Wierwille, *Jesus Christ Is Not God*, p. 79.
2. Victor Paul Wierwille, *The Word's Way*, p. 37.
3. Wierwille, *Jesus Christ Is Not God*, p. 85.
4. *Ibid.*, p. 127,128.
5. *Ibid.*, p. 4.
6. The material used in this dialogue is from taped interviews between members of the Unification Church and students of Northeastern Bible College.
7. Young Oon Kim, *The Divine Principle and Its Application*, p. 75.
8. *The Divine Principle Study Guide*, pp. 139,165,197.

9. *Divine Principle*, p. 212.
10. *Ibid.*, pp. 500,510,520.
11. *Master Speaks* (March and April 1965), MS-3, p. 2.
12. "Freedom of the Press Abused by Berkeley Group: A Rebuttal of False Accusations Against Witness Lee and Local Churches," *The Daily California* (November 29, 1977).
13. Witness Lee, *The Economy of God*, p. 10.
14. Witness Lee, *The Knowledge of Life*, pp. 75,31.
15. Witness Lee, *The Practical Expression of the Church*, p. 43.

GLOSSARY

apostate: one who abandons a religious faith

atone: to make amends for wrong done and thus bring back together those who disagreed

defile: to corrupt the purity or perfection of

deity: the essential nature of a god

desecrate: to profane, treat irreverently

finite: having definite limits, having a limited nature

godhead: the nature of God, especially as existing in three persons but one entity (unity)

incarnation: the union of divinity and humanity in Christ; taking on a human nature

infinite: subject to no limitations

iniquity: sin; wickedness

magi: religious caste to which the Wise Men belonged who came from the East to worship the infant Jesus

Pharisees: one of three chief Jewish parties: believed that religion consists of conformity to the law

preeminence: state of superiority or paramount rank

propitiation: extinguishing of guilt by suffering a penalty or offering a sacrifice

proselyte: (n) in the New Testament, a convert to Judaism; (v) to encourage someone to convert from one religion or belief to another

reconcile: bring together two quarreling parties; restore to friendship or harmony

reconciliation: restoration of harmony between estranged persons

redemption: deliverance from bondage through payment of a ransom price

transgression: sin committed against God

vindicate: to provide justification or defense; protect from attack

BIBLIOGRAPHY OF REFERENCE MATERIALS

Christian Resources

Archer, Gleason. *A Survey of Old Testament Literature.* Chicago, IL: Moody Press, 1964.

Boice, James Montgomery. *God the Redeemer.* Downers Grove, IL: Inter-Varsity Press, 1978.

_____. *The Sovereign God.* Downers Grove, IL: Inter-Varsity Press, 1977.

Bruce, F.F. *The New Testament Documents: Are They Reliable?* Downers Grove, IL: Inter-Varsity Press, 1973.

Brumback, Carl. *God in Three Persons.* Cleveland, TN: Pathway Press, 1959.

Dencher, Ted. *The Watchtower Versus the Bible.* Chicago, IL: Moody Press, 1961.

Fraser, Gordon H. *Is Mormonism Christian?* Chicago, IL: Moody Press, 1977.

Gruss, Edmond Charles. *Apostles of Denial.* Nutley, NJ: Presbyterian and Reformed Publishing Company, 1970.

Hoekema, Anthony A. *The Four Major Cults.* Grand Rapids, MI: Wm. B. Eerdmans Publishing Company, 1963.

Hubbard, David Allan. *What's God Been Doing All This Time?* Glendale, CA: Regal Books, 1970.

Kern, Herbert. *How to Respond to Jehovah's Witnesses.* St. Louis, MO: Concordia Publishing House, 1977.

Little, Paul E. *How to Give Away Your Faith*. Downers Grove, IL: Inter-Varsity Press, 1966.

_____. *Know What You Believe*. Wheaton, IL: Victor Books, 1970.

McDowell, Josh. *Evidence That Demands a Verdict*. Arrowhead Springs, CA: Crusade for Christ, 1972.

_____. *More Evidence That Demands a Verdict*. Arrowhead Springs, CA: Campus Crusade for Christ, 1975.

McElveen, Floyd. *Will the Saints Go Marching In?* Glendale, CA: Regal Books, 1977.

Marshall, Howard I. *Origins of New Testament Christology*. Downers Grove, IL: Inter-Varsity Press, 1976.

_____. *Pocket Guide to Christian Beliefs*. 3rd ed. Downers Grove, IL: Inter-Varsity Press, 1978.

Martin, Walter. *The Maze of Mormonism*. Grand Rapids, MI: Zondervan Publishing House, 1962.

Maeder, Gary with Williams, Don. *The Christian Life: Issues and Answers* Glendale, CA: Regal Books, 1977.

Miller, Chuck. *Now That I'm a Christian*, Volume 1. Glendale, CA: Regal Books. 1975.

Orr, J. Edwin. *100 Questions About God*. Glendale, CA: Regal Books, 1966.

Phillips, J.B. *Your God Is Too Small*. New York, NY: Macmillan Company, 1961.

Ramm, Bernard L. *The God Who Makes a Difference: A Christian Appeal to Reason*. Waco, TX: Word Books, 1972.

Rinker, Rosalind. *You Can Witness with Confidence*. Grand Rapids, MI: Zondervan Publishing House, 1962.

Ropp, Harry L. *The Mormon Papers: Are the Mormon Scriptures Reliable?* Downers Grove, IL: Inter-Varsity Press, 1977.

Schnell, William J. *How to Witness to Jehovah's Witnesses*. Grand Rapids, MI: Baker Books, 1975.

_____. *Jehovah's Witnesses Errors Exposed*. Grand Rapids, MI: Baker Books, 1978.

Stott, John. *Basic Christianity*. Grand Rapids, MI: Wm. B. Eerdmans Company, 1957.

Thomas, Fred W. *Masters of Deception*. Grand Rapids, MI: Baker Books, 1972.

Tope, Wally. *Maximizing Your Witness to Mormons*. "Contemporary Christianity," vol. 7, no. 3, September-November 1977.

Jehovah's Witnesses Resources

The following are published by the Watchtower Bible and Tract Society, Incorporated, Brooklyn, New York.

Russell, Charles Taze. *Studies in the Scriptures*, 1886-1917.

Rutherford, Joseph Franklin. *Intolerance*, 1933.

_____, *The Crisis*, 1933.

_____, *The Harp of God*, 1927.

The following publications of the Watchtower Bible and Tract Society, Incorporated, Brooklyn, New York reflect the Jehovah's Witnesses' policy of anonymous publication.

Aid to Bible Understanding, 1971.

Awake!, several issues.

From Paradise Lost to Paradise Regained, 1958.

Jehovah's Witnesses in the Divine Purpose, 1959.

Let God Be True, Revised Edition, 1952.

Let Your Name Be Sanctified, 1961.

Life Everlasting in Freedom of the Sons of God, 1966.

Make Sure of All Things, 1953, revised 1957.

New Heavens and a New Earth, 1953.

Qualified to Be Ministers, 1955.

The Kingdom Is at Hand, 1944.

Theocratic Aid to Kingdom Publishers, 1945.

The Truth Shall Make You Free, 1943.

The Truth That Leads to Eternal Life, 1968.

"The Word" Who Is He? According to John, 1962.

The Watchtower, various issues.

Things in Which It Is Impossible for God to Lie, 1965.

What Has Religion Done for Mankind?, 1951.

Yearbook of Jehovah's Witnesses, several issues.

You May Survive Armageddon into God's New World, 1955.

Your Will Be Done on Earth, 1958.

Mormon Resources

_____. *Book of Mormon*. Salt Lake City, UT: Church of Jesus Christ of Latter-day Saints.

_____. *Dialogue: A Journal of Mormon Thought*. Salt Lake City, UT: Church of Jesus Christ of Latter-day Saints.

_____. *Doctrine and Covenants*. Salt Lake City, UT: Church of Jesus Christ of Latter-day Saints, 1968.

_____. *Documentary History of the Church*. Salt Lake City, UT: Deseret Book Company, 1971.

_____. *Journal of Discourses*. Salt Lake City, UT: Church of Jesus Christ of Latter-day Saints. Continuing publication.

_____. "Millennial Star." Mormon periodical.

_____. *Pearl of Great Price*. First issued by James E. Talmage in 1902.

_____. "Times and Seasons." Mormon periodical. First issued in Commerce, Illinois, November 1839.

Carter, Kate. *Denominations That Base Their Beliefs on the Teachings of Joseph Smith*, (pamphlet). Published by the author, 1962.

Hunter, Milton R. *Gospel Through the Ages*. Salt Lake City, UT: Deseret Book Company, 1945.

McConkie, Bruce. "What Mormons Think of Christ" (tract). Salt Lake City, UT: Deseret News Press, no date.

McMurrin, Sterling M. *The Philosophical Foundations of Mormon Theology*. Salt Lake City: University of Utah Press, 1959.

Pratt, Orson. "The Seer." Periodical first published Washington, D.C., January 1853.

Smith, Joseph Fielding. *Doctrines of Salvation.* Salt Lake City, UT: Bookcraft, 1954.

Smith, Joseph Fielding, compiler. *Teachings of the Prophet Joseph Smith.* Salt Lake City, UT: Deseret Book Company, 1976.

Stewart, Ora Pate. *We Believe.* Salt Lake City, UT: Bookcraft, 1954.

Talmage, James E. *A Study of the Articles of Faith.* Salt Lake City, UT: The Church of Jesus Christ of Latter-day Saints, 1968.

Resources for Glossary

Gehman, Henry Snyder, ed. *The New Westminster Dictionary of the Bible.* Philadelphia: The Westminster Press, 1970.

Webster's New Collegiate Dictionary. Springfield, MA: G. & S. Merriam Co., 1973.

Other Resources

Kim, Young Oon. *Divine Principle and Its Application.* Washington, D.C.: The Holy Spirit Association for Unification of World Christianity, 1968.

_____. *The Divine Principle Study Guide.* Washington, D.C.: The Holy Spirit Association for Unification of World Christianity, 1968.

Lee, Witness. *The Economy of God.* Los Angeles, CA: Stream Publishers, 1968.

_____. *The Knowledge of Life.* Los Angeles, CA: Stream Publishers, 1973.

_____. *The Practical Expression of the Church.* Los Angeles, CA: Stream Publishers, 1970.

Wierwille, Victor Paul. *Jesus Christ Is Not God.* New Knoxville, Ohio: The American Christian Press, 1975.

_____. *The Word's Way.* New Knoxville, Ohio: The American Christian Press, 1971.